Common Sense Selling

A New Look At How Successful Salespeople Sell

By
Jim Dunn
&
John Schumann

Third Edition
San Diego, CA

Common Sense Selling

Published by SalesCoach, LLC
3934 Murphy Canyon Road, #B200
San Diego, CA 92123
Tel: (800) 235-2816

ISBN Number
1-59196-573-X

Printed in the U. S. A.

Table of Contents

Introduction

"Rowing harder doesn't help
if the boat is headed in the wrong direction."
Kenichi Ohmae, business strategy coach

What if everything you believed about selling was untrue? What if the usual way of selling was really the hard way? Suppose what seemed to be the hard way to sell was, in the long run, the easiest and best way to sell? This book is about the various strategies that are employed by "buyers" and "sellers."

In the following pages many myths about selling will be exposed that have held salespeople back for years, in some cases causing them to doubt whether they even belonged in the sales profession. These long-held beliefs and attitudes have created a dysfunctional sales process that alienates buyers, frustrates sellers and has given the selling profession a bad name. Many approach selling with fear. Employment opportunities often are qualified by the words "no selling required." Telemarketers tell us they are not selling anything.

Most books on selling, though well-intended, are one-dimensional. They focus on only one aspect of a very complicated subject. This book is designed to provide you with an overview of the most important concepts in selling. From dealing successfully with people to developing strategies and skills; from managing your sales process to managing your attitude, we hope to provide you, the reader, with revolutionary concepts so you can take a huge step in your journey toward mastering the art of selling. And, it is an art. Make no mistake about that.

The successful salesperson must be adept at interpersonal relationships, communication, psychology, detective work, product knowledge, problem solving and managing multiple projects simultaneously. And this all takes place in an atmosphere of distrust, rejection and immense pressure to perform. If there's a tougher business, I don't know what it is. The failure rate is extremely high, yet the rewards are unequalled for the few who are really successful.

We'll address the issue of why all selling environments are not the same, so the skills needed for one may not be applicable in another. With few exceptions, many salespeople begin their careers in simple, transactional selling, and progress to more complex, relationship sales as time goes by. This book addresses that situation.

We know that to be successful in sales requires hard work and attention to detail. Some of the material contained herein will not be new to you, but some of it will. So if we tell you something you already know, you're on the right path. Keep in mind that selling is a *slight edge* business. One little thing that you do differently, one minor change in your approach, one new idea, can be the difference between getting the sale or finishing second. Second place pays poorly. Saying "we came close" doesn't pay the mortgage or buy the new BMW.

"Professional selling" is an oxymoron, in most cases. Professionals work hard at their craft, take the time to seek out new methods to do things better so that they can stay ahead of the pack. Sadly, most salespeople approach their profession as a temporary stop until something better comes along. They take shortcuts, avoid opportunities to improve their skills, and hope that they will succeed in spite of their lack of commitment. By virtue of the fact that you have decided to devote some time to reading this book, you probably are in the minority, and we congratulate you.

We've tried to follow the KISS principle (Keep It Short and Simple) in writing this book. We've attempted to present you with the most important nuggets and eliminate the detail that might confuse.

We use primarily the masculine pronoun only because it is customary to do so. Certainly we do not intend to be sexist. And since the words "product" and "service" are so often interchangeable, we usually mean either or both whenever we refer to one or the other.

One final thought. The last chapter is a narrative of how the Common Sense Selling® process might be implemented in a real world sales opportunity. You might want to read it first, then read the rest of the book, then go back to the narrative again. I think that after reading the book this story will bring all the concepts together for you and help you gain a more complete understanding of how the process works.

Enjoy the book, play the game to win…and good selling.

Chapter 1
A Sales Autopsy

(While this narrative is about selling a service to retailers, you will undoubtedly see the parallels to selling your products and services. Our experience in training throughout many different industries shows that while the product or service may be different, the game is essentially the same.)

Some years ago, back when I was in corporate America, I worked for an inventory service company. We counted inventory for retailers and we were the second largest inventory service in the country. We were the Avis of inventory services, if you will. I was in charge of sales and marketing for the company and was responsible for developing relationships with the major chain retailers. As such, my key prospects were companies like Kmart, Sears, Toys R Us, Home Depot, The Limited apparel chain, Rite Aid and other major retail chains that are household words today.

Like most salespeople, I maintained a list of my top prospects, the companies that were really key to the growth of our business. Many of these retailers were customers of our largest competitor, which was about three times our size in sales, but that was the only advantage they had over us. We were certainly competitive in our ability to service nationwide retailers like these.

"We're thinking about making a change."

I don't know about you, but I found it difficult to break through the barriers that these large prospects erected to keep salespeople out. It was tough dealing with those gatekeepers. You can imagine my surprise when one day I got a call from a very large retailer based in New York stating, "We're currently using your number one competitor and we're thinking about making a change. We've heard good things about your company. Would you be interested in coming out to see us?" This company had over 1000 stores nationally and was a subsidiary of the nation's largest apparel chain, one of the companies that was on my "top 10" prospect list. I was very excited to receive a call like this; it seemed to be a great opportunity, since it's not often a prospect calls you to set up an appointment. This appeared to be a chance to not only get a new client, but also to gain an entrée into the parent corporation, and an opportunity to develop business with their other subsidiaries.

"Lately there have been a few problems and we're looking for some alternatives."

I flew to New York for the meeting. Shortly after we sat down, they said, "Our relationship with ABC Company (my competitor) has been pretty good over the years, but lately there have been a few problems, and we're looking for some alternatives." Here's what I knew about my competitor: when they had a long, exclusive relationship with a client, often their service would start to deteriorate and their prices would begin to escalate. Naturally I assumed that this was the case in this situation.

We talked for a while longer and I found out how many stores they had, when they took inventory, etc. I discovered all the information that I needed to understand the technical requirements of their inventory program and determined that they spent about $3 million dollars a year on inventory services. That figure was attractive to us since at the time our annual sales were about $75 million. If you considered the potential with the parent corporation and all its subsidiaries, their revenue potential was in the $30 million dollar range; a prospect with enormous potential for us.

"If your service is good, we'll give you very serious consideration as a business partner."

Then they said to me, "Here's what we'd like to do. We'd like you to do about 15 inventories for us - free of charge, of course. It will be a good opportunity for us to evaluate the quality of your service, and it will give you a chance to see how we prepare stores for inventory and what kind of counting productivity you can get in the stores. And if your service is good, we can probably do some business."

It would cost us about $45,000 do these inventories, but we often did one or two free inventories with a new prospect before we had signed a contract. It gave us a great opportunity to put our best crews into the stores and really demonstrate our competence, and it also helped us understand how many pieces of apparel we could count hourly - information that we'd need when it came time to consider how much we would have to charge them. Even when considering the up front cost to the company, these "evaluation" inventories were a good investment for us, considering the overall potential.

"These were the best inventories we've ever seen. If your fees are competitive, we can give you some business."

After the meeting I flew back home and put together the plan for doing the evaluation inventories. Several weeks later, they were completed. From our perspective, the inventories had gone well and I called the customer to get their input. They expressed complete satisfaction, going so far as to say that we had done "the best inventories they'd ever seen." They asked me to develop a fee proposal for them stating, "If your fees are competitive, we can give you some business."

Let's take a step back and evaluate the situation. They called me, stating they were having some problems with their current vendor and were thinking about making a change. From a salesperson's perspective, it doesn't get much better than this. Most salespeople would forecast this as a "done deal." I suspect that if you were in my shoes, you'd feel the same. When I tell this story in our workshops, 95% of the attendees think this is going to be a "slam dunk." Now let's continue with the story to see what happens.

The next step was to develop the fee proposal. I tried to maintain our normal profitability for this type of account, avoiding a low-ball pricing strategy because I felt that price was not a major issue in their decision. Several days later I flew to New York to make the presentation.

To this day I recall the meeting vividly, even though it was a number of years ago. Our company's strategy on these types of proposals to major prospects was to do a complete "dog and pony show." We reasoned that when you do a proposal for $3 million dollars, you don't just give them a piece of paper with the fee on it. We had a standard "proposal book" which contained about ten sections of information, including pictures and bios of the senior management team, the story about how the company was founded, maps of the locations of our 120 offices nationwide, a client list, testimonials, etc. (It was very "exciting" stuff.) The last section contained the fee proposal.

I recall being about five minutes into the presentation, no doubt talking enthusiastically about the experience of our management team, when they started thumbing their way through the other sections. Clearly, they wanted to get to the section that had the most interest for them – the price.

"You can save us 15%!"

I've seen buyers use "the flinch" many times when the salesperson tells them the price and, while this wasn't the classic flinch, they were quite visibly surprised when they saw our pricing model. Our prices were about 15% lower than they were paying their current vendor, an annual savings of $450,000, a savings that goes right to their bottom line. This price disparity surprised me as well. I believed we'd be lower than our competitor, but not 15% lower. Nevertheless, I had no regrets because our prices would give us a fair profit margin. I didn't feel like I had "left any money on the table."

Let's evaluate the situation to this point.
- *They initiated contact with me.*
- *They expressed some level of dissatisfaction with my competitor.*
- *They acknowledged that our service was exceptional.*
- *We could save them 15% - $450,000 per year!*

Looks like a sure thing!

Full of enthusiasm and confidence, I went for the close. "We're pleased that this proposal meets your needs and are ready to be a part of your inventory program starting with your next inventory cycle in January. Based on your pricing and your satisfaction with our service, how much of your program are you prepared to give to us?," I asked, secretly hoping for a commitment of 35-40% of the business as a start.

Their response went something like this: "This is a great proposal. We really need a little time to look it over and see how it fits with our whole inventory program. We're pleased with how responsive you've been. Obviously your pricing is excellent. We have a couple of other people in the department who we want to review your proposal and will do that in the next few days. We'll call you sometime next week after we've spoken with them. Okay?"

I had hoped to get a commitment before I left, but given the circumstances reasoned that since our pricing had been better than they expected, perhaps they needed to delay a decision in order to consider committing a larger piece of their business to us. *(Most salespeople, being optimistic and trusting by nature, think like this.)* I'd certainly heard stalls like this before and knew that often prospects are reluctant to make commitments quickly. But I was very optimistic that we would get this business given all the positive indicators that I'd seen. Smiling and shaking hands with everyone, I left the meeting and said I was looking forward to speaking with them again in a week or so.

I remember that as soon as I left the meeting I called my boss to tell him how well the proposal was received. On the plane back home I recall thinking how pleased everyone at the company was going to be when we got a nice chunk of this business. It was a good flight.

The following week I waited patiently for their call, but it didn't come. I rationalized that people get busy with meetings and travel commitments and assumed that they simply hadn't had a chance to get together to discuss my proposal further. But I was taught that persistence is the hallmark of a good salesperson, so I called them to follow up. It seemed they were always in meetings. (Perhaps they were trying to decide how much business to give us?) My calls went unreturned despite the fact that I called regularly. Invariably an administrative person who assured me they would call back right away dutifully took my message, but they called back. My enthusiasm began to wane; fear, uncertainty and doubt began to set in. It was not a good feeling. Perhaps you, the reader, can relate to this.

What's going on here?

When I finally reached them about three weeks later, my worst fears were realized. They said that they felt it was only fair to give the incumbent vendor, my competitor, a chance to respond to my proposal since they'd had such a great relationship with them over the years. (In retrospect, I think the relationship improved dramatically after I got involved.) Of course, my competitor responded. They beat my quote by a "fraction," I was told, in return for an exclusive on the business for two years. So I was shut out and my competitor had to reduce their prices by 15%. And the customer saved almost a million dollars over two years without even having to take a risk by changing suppliers.

Who really was the winner? It certainly wasn't my company. We had invested approximately $50,000 and a great deal of my most important resource, my time, and we came up empty.

Although my competitor retained the business, he did so at greatly reduced margins. That $450,000 that they "spent" to retain the business came right off their bottom line and went straight to the prospect's bottom line. The big winner was the prospect, of course, netting a $450,000 annual saving and 15 free inventories.

Was I set up?

Let's do an autopsy. Do you think that the prospect's renegotiation with their current vendor was an afterthought? Or, was it pre-planned?

If you guessed it was pre-planned, you're probably right. If that wasn't the case, you can bet that sometime during the process someone in management suggested that they contact their current vendor to see what they could do. In any event, they had used me to negotiate a better deal with the current vendor. They held out the bait and I went for it...hook, line and sinker. They were in control of the entire process and I was their innocent victim.

This story is not intended to disparage prospects, not by a long shot. In fact, I know that sometimes I play one potential vendor off against another. That's just being a smart buyer. But it does illustrate the dilemma that most salespeople face on a daily basis.

The prospect won because his strategy was more effective than mine!

The only positive outcome from this experience was that I learned an important lesson. I learned that this prospect had a strategy going in, and it was more effective than my selling strategy. If they had hired a consultant to come in to save them nearly a million dollars on their inventory program over two years they probably couldn't have found anyone better than me to do the job. And I actually paid for the privilege. That more than fits the description of an "unpaid consultant."

If you're like most salespeople, you probably lost track of the number of times this has happened to you over the years. Prospects have a system that they use with salespeople, and it's very effective. This book is about the various strategies that are employed by both buyers and sellers. I think you'll find it enlightening. And if you're tired of being an unpaid consultant, you'll find some very effective strategies here to put you back in control of the sales process and win more business.

Key Points
1. Don't believe everything your prospect says.
2. The person with the best process usually wins.
3. Be skeptical when it looks like an easy sale.
4. Don't make assumptions.

Chapter 2
The Changing Face of Selling

You should <u>not</u> use the same strategies and tactics to sell a complex, high tech solution that you would use to sell a simple, low tech product such as furniture, cell phones or even cars.

At our seminars we often ask participants if selling has changed. The answer is always the same, "You bet it has. It's gotten much harder." While that may be true, it fails to get to the root of the problem.

Years ago, the typical sale was transactional in nature. Small dollar deals were consummated in one meeting. Products were seen as commodities and were sold that way. The pressure on the seller was tremendous since he knew he usually had but one chance to close the deal. If he didn't get the business, his competitor would. Faced with that challenge, sellers were trained to use manipulative techniques in an attempt to gain the upper hand.

Selling has, indeed, become more difficult. Today the typical sale has become more relationship oriented and far more complex. The reasons for this are:

- The typical sale has become larger in dollar terms.
- Buyers have become more sophisticated.
- The impact of a poor buying decision becomes greater as the dollar amount of the sale increases.
- With greater risk, companies often involve more people in the decision process, which extends the sales cycle.
- The relationship between the vendor and the client often continues for some period of time, perhaps indefinitely.
- Trust is a critical factor in the relationship.

The role of the salesperson has evolved from product pusher to consultant and creative problem solver. Unfortunately for the profession, the skills of the typical salesperson have not evolved at nearly the same rate as the complexity of the sale.

The Transactional Sale

Traditional closing techniques attempt to manipulate the buyer because the seller feels like he has one chance to close the sale and if the buyer "escapes" without the sale being consummated, the seller knows he will likely not have another chance with the buyer. The seller has learned that when the buyer begs off with the ubiquitous, "I'll be back," 98% of the time he does not return. Traditional closing techniques are ineffective or, at worst, have a negative impact on the sale when a trusting relationship between buyer and seller is important.

While selling has generally become more complex and relationship oriented, there are still many products and services that are transactional sales.

Characteristics of a transactional sale are:

- The sale is won or lost in one brief meeting between buyer and seller.
- The product or service is seen as a commodity.
- Price and availability are prime buying factors.
- There is usually only one person making the decision.
- The impact of a bad decision will have little, if any, lasting effect.
- The dollar value of the sale is typically, but not always, low.
- The buyer is well informed of the features and benefits of the product or service.
- The buyer does not need to trust the salesperson, although friendliness and trust never hurt.

A few examples of a transactional sale are:
- In-home direct sales like vacuum cleaners, water treatment systems, etc.
- Long distance telephone service.
- Automobiles (despite the high dollar value of the sale).
- Most retail sales.
- Products sold by telemarketers.
- Insurance (basic auto, homeowners and some lower value life policies).

Traditional closes associated with transactional sales are:
- "If I could show you a way to solve the problem, would you buy it today?"
- "Will that be cash or charge?" (Alternative choice close.)
- "If I could guarantee delivery by the 15th of the month, are you prepared to approve the paperwork today?" (The sharp angle close.)
- "What do I need to do to earn your business today?" (Still being used on the car lots of America.)
- "When you consider that the investment breaks down to less than a dollar a day, surely you wouldn't deprive your wife of the pleasure of _____ for that insignificant amount, would you?" (Reduced to the ridiculous close.)
- "My dear old mother, who means a great deal to me, used to say that silence means consent. Is that what you mean?" (Yes, you can still find this stuff on the bookshelves. This "clever" ploy, called the My Dear Old Mother close, was developed by one of America's most famous sales trainers who suggests that you use it when the prospect is not responding to a closing question.)

- "That wise old statesman, Benjamin Franklin, used to use a kind of balance sheet when he was undecided about something. On one side he'd write down "yes" and on the other "no." Next, he'd list all the reasons for going ahead and then the reasons not to. Whichever side weighed heavier would be the one he'd go with. Let's do that. I'll help you. Let's look at all the reasons for buying the product today." (Called the Ben Franklin close, the salesperson is very helpful on the "yes" side, but remains quiet on the "no" side, insuring that there are more "yes's" than "no's." Pretty clever, right? Ben's probably turning in his grave.)

Ask yourself how well these closes would work with you? I'll bet you've heard everyone of them before. Clearly, they put a lot of pressure on the buyer to make the purchase - *now*. That's okay if you will never see the buyer again. In fact, it's not a bad strategy.

Let's assume for a moment that you are a senior VP with a company and you are buying a $150,000 hardware and software package to improve the company's ability to process employee payroll. Would these closes be effective or put you off?

The Complex Sale

While the transactional sale will always be with us, more and more of the selling opportunities that we encounter these days are complex and require a strong relationship between the buyer and seller to be successful.

Characteristics of a complex sale are:

- Relationship and trust are very important criteria in selecting a vendor partner.
- Price and availability are secondary concerns when choosing a vendor.

- Making a bad decision can be very costly, so exploring options becomes more important.
- The buyer depends on the salesperson to professionally diagnose the problem and recommend a workable solution; therefore, the salesperson must be a skilled investigator.
- Solutions are often customized for the buyer – a generic, off the shelf solution usually doesn't work.
- The decision process can be lengthy and involve numerous people because the decision impacts many people and departments.

Summary – Simple to Complex

Simple Sale (Transactional)		Complex Sale (Relationship)
Retail	*Examples*	B 2 B
Low value	*$ size of sale*	Big bucks
Usually just one	*# people involved*	Several
Short, one call	*Sales cycle*	Long, many calls
Minimal	*Risk of making a bad decision*	Mistakes can be very costly
Not important	*Importance of trust*	Very important

The skills needed for the two types of sales are diametrically opposed. Skills that work well in one type of sale can be a detriment in the other.

Skills Needed

Simple Sale	Complex Sale
Product knowledge	Managing a complex process
"Gift of gab"	Questioning skills
Persuading	Listening skills
Overcoming objections	Building trust & rapport
Hard closing	Problem solving

The differences are dramatic, yet there is a lot of gray area in between the two extremes, as we'll see in the hybrid sale.

The Hybrid Sale

Obviously, it's not always easy to determine what type of sale you are in. One of our clients, a distributor of valves and fittings, is in both types of sales. Initially, they must open the account and that's a relationship sale. The dollar volume of the account may exceed several million dollars a year and the seller provides educational and consultative services to the client. They have relationships with the client that cross departmental lines and span from front line staff to the senior VP level. With some of these larger accounts they are seen as a partner, not a vendor. In addition, they have smaller customers who use several vendors and purchase more transactionally. Their salespeople need to have the skills to operate in both worlds, but the real payoff is in the relationship sale.

Where Are You?

The real question is, what type of sale are you in? Purely transactional or purely complex, or perhaps something that is a bit of both? The more your selling environment tends to be complex, the less effective the traditional, manipulative, aggressive closes will be, and the greater the need to avoid the traditional sales techniques in favor of the consultative, relationship approach that works best in the higher value sale.

Key Points
1. Selling is changing; it's becoming more complex.
2. Transactional selling skills are a liability in a complex sale where relationship and trust are important.

Chapter 3
Attitude Adjustment

Common Sense Selling® is a counterintuitive approach to the way most people sell. The ideas in this chapter will undoubtedly fly in the face of much of what you've been told about selling. Unfortunately, most of what you've been told doesn't work in complex sales. Keep an open mind when reading this chapter and you will have some "light bulb" moments.

Bad Attitudes

Too many salespeople show up with an attitude. It sounds like this. "I've got the best solution available, and my job is to convince my prospects that I'm right. To do this I will offer a precise, logical argument supported by as much data as necessary to prove my point. I will become skillful at overcoming their objections and if they don't buy, I will be persistent and follow up relentlessly until I win their business." This is the "try harder" syndrome. Give points for effort, but not for effectiveness. This attitude just doesn't work well any longer.

Contrast this with an entirely different attitude. "I believe strongly in my product or service. But, I realize that not everyone is a prospect for what I sell. And I realize that the harder I try to sell, the less receptive my prospect will be. Therefore, my best strategy is to encourage the prospect tell me about his/her situation without being afraid that I might take advantage of them. Coming to a point of understanding without the pressure of trying to sell will meet both the prospect's needs and my company's needs most effectively."

Put yourself in the prospect's shoes. Which salesperson would you prefer to deal with; the aggressive one or the inquisitive one? Which attitude would encourage the most trust? Which attitude takes the pressure off both the buyer and the seller? Obviously, the less aggressive attitude is preferable since it removes the pressure.

Misunderstandings

For years selling focused on making enthusiastic, detailed presentations. To that end, product knowledge was key. Companies invested heavily in teaching their salespeople product knowledge, at the expense of selling skills. It's estimated that roughly 80% of the training salespeople receive is product knowledge oriented. Clearly skill training has taken a back seat to product training.

SALESPERSON'S DISEASE

Picture this: XZY Software, Inc. has brought their entire sales force into their headquarters for three days of intensive product training on the latest version of their

24

software. They're shown how to demo the product, taught all the features, specifications, applications, etc. At the end of the three days they're experts. Imagine what's likely to happen on the first sales call they make after training. Unless the prospect beats them to the point with, "What's new with your software?" they're likely to lead with, "Let me tell you about our newest release. It's got (feature A, feature B and feature C), and here's how it can help you solve (problem A, problem B and problem C)." The focus on teaching product knowledge takes the focus off qualifying and asking questions. As such, this "premature presentation," as you will learn, will hurt you more than it will help you.

When skill training was considered necessary, it focused on overcoming objections and closing, for a very good reason: product pushers whose selling strategy was to overwhelm the prospect with the features and benefits of their offering needed those skills desperately. However, there's an underlying concept that is often overlooked: sales pitches sometimes provide prospects with "ammunition" they can use to create objections. For example, if the salesperson starts discussing features, specifications, pricing, etc. it's possible for the prospect to find something that might compare unfavorably to the product he's currently using. On the contrary, if you limit the amount of information that you give, it's more difficult for the prospect to find something to object to. Clearly, investigative skills are more important than presentation skills in today's selling environment that rewards the problem solver, not the product pusher.

Another misunderstanding is that the entire selling process has to be adversarial. Both parties seem to feel like they must gain the upper hand and not let the other take advantage of them. Feeling you have been taken advantage of leads to resentment and possible retribution at some point in the future. This is not a good foundation for a long-term business relationship. Years and years of manipulation by both parties have caused this unfortunate imbalance in the typical sales process.

When a sale is made, both parties must win or they shouldn't do business together. Selling has to become a cooperative effort. To make this happen, the salesperson must put the prospect at ease and stress the fact that their mutual objective should be to exchange enough information to find out if there is a reason to start a business relationship. And, that if it doesn't look like a fit, either party has the right to disengage. (In Chapter 8 you'll learn how to control the sales environment with meeting agreements.) The focus of qualifying should be for the salesperson to ask questions about the business challenges the prospect wants to resolve, not on what the seller has to offer. At the end of the process, the seller will make his recommendations based on the answers to his qualifying questions and the prospect will give the seller a decision. No manipulation will be necessary by either party to gain an advantage.

"Killer" Beliefs In a Relationship Sale

Here's a summary of the beliefs that salespeople have that will do them more harm than good in a complex sale where a trusting relationship is important.

I need to educate my prospect; presentation skills are my most effective tool. Premature presentations are the biggest challenge salespeople face today. Let's face it, no one ever lost a sale by listening too much. When you're educating, you're talking. When you're talking it's difficult to understand your prospect's challenges and he will realize that and conclude that you bring little value to the relationship. Your job is to qualify your prospect and investigative skills are your most effective tool.

Everyone needs what I sell; hearing "no" is a failure. If you feel that "no" is a failure, you'll resist it at all costs, creating a pressure filled atmosphere that will turn a skeptical prospect into a defensive prospect who's main objective is to get rid of you. If you believe that everybody needs what you sell, it's difficult to be objective. The buyer will conclude that your self-interest is greater than your desire to help. A more productive belief is that not everyone is a prospect for what I sell and "no" is not a failure as long as I've qualified the opportunity adequately.

When the prospect says, "I need to think it over," there's still a chance. Many "think it over's" are just slow "no's" with a free torture treatment. Prospects rarely say "no" to salespeople even when they have little or no intention to buy. They believe that it is polite not to hurt the salesperson's feelings or they want to avoid the pressure that they feel the salesperson will apply when rejected. Sometimes prospects won't say "no" simply so they can bring the salesperson back to pick their brains for more information. Instead, you'll be put in the chase mode, making a long sales cycle even longer. You should be skeptical (not reassured) when your prospect tells you that he needs to "think it over."

My features and benefits differentiate me from my competitors; they give me an advantage. Face it, most salespeople show up with the same tired old platitudes ('we have the best quality in the industry, our service is outstanding and our prices are very competitive"). It's called "fluff." If you rely on features and benefits, you're probably going to sound just like everybody else, and your prospect may conclude that what you sell is just a commodity. When you're perceived as a commodity, price becomes the most important buying criteria. Bad news for you.

27

My job is to convince my prospect that he would benefit from purchasing from me; I need to be a good closer. This is an antiquated belief and bound to lead to resistance. Following this belief will encourage you to put pressure on the prospect to buy. People resist pressure in a relationship sale; it's just human nature. The prospect's job to convince you that he has a problem, the budget and the decision-making ability to fix it and needs your help. Try this attitude on your next sales interview and see how it will change your approach.

Financial considerations are the most important factor in determining who gets the business. This belief puts the emphasis on price and that's not what you want. Price is very seldom the real issue in a complex sale. Conviction that you can help them solve their problem and get a return on their investment is the bottom line. If you can help them increase their business or save them money, your price is relative to their gain.

If my prospects like me, they will buy from me. Trust and rapport are important but the real issue is whether or not the prospect thinks you can solve their problem. If they do, you're likely to get the business.

If you look at the common denominator in these beliefs, the focus has to be shifted to *qualifying*, not selling.

Key Points
1. Your attitudes and beliefs are very important; they dictate what you do and how you do it. Ultimately, your attitudes and beliefs control your results.
2. Hearing "no" is not a failure; not everyone is a prospect for your product or service.
3. You should believe in the Law of Abundance – there's plenty of business out there. Don't hang on to a

prospective client when the odds of being successful are slim. Find another opportunity.

Chapter 4
The Buyer's Seduction

A Case Study

Howard is a physician friend of ours who runs a large pathology department in a well-known healthcare network. He had some serious issues with a software package that helped his department communicate with the physicians in the network, a function that was critical to ensure superior patient care.

Wanting to rectify the situation, Howard asked Bill, the administrative manager of the lab, to check out some options so they could find a solution. Although Bill disliked dealing with salespeople, he immediately went to work on the problem. He contacted three companies and soon had appointments with each prospective vendor. The budget for the purchase was $250,000.

Because this looked like a big opportunity with a high visibility healthcare provider, each salesperson showed up for their appointment with a systems engineer in tow. Bill, whose main interest was to gather enough information to put together a really good recommendation for Howard, went on the offensive. He was careful to explain that although he was not the ultimate decision maker, his recommendations would carry a great deal of weight with Howard. He told them that he was going to evaluate several vendors and that pricing would be a key element in their final decision. Being suspicious of all salespeople, he was reluctant to divulge too much information. Of course, Bill asked them many questions and after three meetings with two vendors and four with the other, he was a subject matter expert himself and felt like he really had the situation under control. For the vendors, each of the three undoubtedly considered that the information they provided

Bill was an advantage for them. At this point, almost three months had elapsed and everybody was anxious to get the deal done.

Two weeks later Bill had proposals from all three. The tentative decision was made to accept the proposal from most expensive vendor, but there was one more move to be made. The preferred vendor was invited to meet with Bill and Howard. They explained that while they felt his proposal was the one they wanted to go with, it was difficult to justify the 15% price premium between him and the other vendors. Could he help them out, they wondered? After some negotiating, the price was reduced by 10% and the deal was consummated.

The Prospect's Game: A Seduction Strategy

The following is the way many prospects deal with salespeople. You'll no doubt recognize the strategy. The basis for this approach is two-fold; you, the salesperson, have information that can help them improve their knowledge and evaluate options more effectively, but they don't trust you (remember, you're in sales).

So they may express interest in what you're offering, holding out the carrot to you as an inducement to provide them with the information they want. They may even embellish their interest somewhat in order to get you to do some "pro bono consulting." (Have you ever been seduced by comments like, "we've heard good things about your company," "we're thinking about making a change," "we're evaluating other vendors," etc.)? It's pretty exciting when those comments are made to you by a prospective buyer, isn't it? It seems, to the unsuspecting salesperson, that the need to ask many qualifying questions is eliminated, doesn't it?

However, although they are expressing interest, they are rather hesitant to provide you with much information, fearing that you may use that information to sell them something that they don't need or pressure them into making a premature decision. Instead, they continue the seduction process with comments and questions such as, "our current vendor has had some problems lately," "how would you address a problem like this?," "can we see a demo?," "when can we see a proposal?," etc. Guess who's doing all the talking now? That's right, the salesperson. But, who is controlling the process? Right again – the prospect.

The last one, asking for a proposal, is the ultimate seduction. They'll ask for one, even if they have little interest in using your products or services. After all, the proposal is free, and they know you'd be disappointed if you didn't have the chance to make a presentation. Wouldn't you?

When you deliver the proposal, they typically decline to make a decision saying they need time to evaluate it or consult with others in the company. Often, they appear enthusiastic ("thanks a lot for the proposal," "looks good," etc.), but this is simply good manners and, perhaps unintentionally, a way to keep you feeling positive about the opportunity so that you won't put pressure on them to buy. It does have the additional benefit (to them, of course) of keeping you in the game so that you can continue to be a "pro bono" consulting resource. Sometimes they even promise to "call you in a few days" with a decision, but that's a promise that's frequently broken.

During this "evaluation period," they tend to be doing one of two things. Often they go "shopping," asking your competitors including, of course, the incumbent vendor if they can "do better." It's a blatant attempt to improve their situation, at your expense. Occasionally they do nothing because they were not serious about buying in the first place.

Finally, when it's clear in their mind who will be given the business (not you), they avoid your calls. Or, if you were lucky enough to actually reach them, they make the excuse that they need more time. More often than not, they never say "no." Eventually, and experience tells them this will happen, you will lose interest and stop calling.

Does this sound familiar? Of course it does. What would motivate the prospect to use this system? The answer is simple…a desire to get information and to stay in control. It's very effective for the prospect, but not so effective for you.

Fortunately you, the salesperson, are not entirely without a strategy to deal with the buyer, are you? Of course not. You've been taught to ask questions, probe for needs, talk about budgets and get in front of the decision maker, haven't you? Sure you have, but in spite of all that training, 85% of you don't do a very effective job in this critical area. In fact, most salespeople do a very poor job of qualifying. Maybe it's not your fault, considering that your training relies heavily on pitching the compelling reasons (features & benefits) for someone to choose you over the competition. And the buyer takes control by turning you into an unpaid consultant.

How do salespeople typically respond? Salespeople are always on the hunt for qualified prospects and are eager to qualify as many potential buyers as possible. Generally speaking that's a laudable attribute; however, salespeople also spend far too much time in front of unqualified prospects. Quantity, not quality, seems to be the objective. Don't you want to provide big numbers when asked, "How many prospects do you have in your pipeline?" by your sales manager?

As a result, sellers take shortcuts in the qualifying process, subconsciously believing that if they ask too many qualifying questions, they might discover that this "suspect" really isn't a prospect. Ignorance is bliss, as they say. Thus, anyone who requests a presentation or invites you in or agrees to meet with you, anyone who buys from a competitor, anyone who loosely fits the description of a current customer or anyone who simply has a pulse seems to be "qualified." Salespeople are notoriously bad at qualifying.

They are, however, very good at presenting. Here's where beliefs enter the picture, creating problems for salespeople. Most salespeople believe selling is all about presenting the compelling reasons why a prospect should select their company. Attempting to build credibility, they place their trust in an antiquated selling methodology called "feature & benefit" selling. Confidently extolling the virtues of their company and their offering, they spout tired old platitudes like, "we're a leader in the industry," "our customer satisfaction level is 95%," "we've got leading edge...," etc. Sound familiar? These statements could be, and are, made by any number of companies. Whether or not they are true is irrelevant. They certainly don't ring true for the buyer, having heard the same thing from everybody who is trying to make the sale.

Do you see the problem this creates? Everybody sounds the same. When that happens, the buyer sees you and your competition as a commodity. That's why feature and benefit selling is antiquated; it "commoditizes" what you sell and forces price to become the major criteria in the selection process. Focusing on your features and benefits also reduces your ability to discover the buyer's needs, since you're spending valuable time talking and not listening.

Here's another problem. Once you have "dumped" your information, done the "dog and pony" show, there's only one thing left to do – ask for the business. That's right – close. You can't go back and ask more qualifying questions; you've lost the right to do that. Now things start to get sticky. The seller is trying to close and the buyer doesn't want to be closed. Instead of a "yes" the seller hears stalls and objections. "We're not ready quite yet," "we need some time to think this over," "I'll have to check with my boss," "it looks good, but .....," "the prices are a little higher than we want to pay." You've heard all these put-offs before.

BUYERS MISLEAD SALESPEOPLE

Frantically, the intrepid salesperson heaps on more features and benefits, perhaps even offers some price concessions, but these ploys seldom work. Although frustrated, the salesperson believes he's still in the game since he didn't get the "no" he was afraid of. In fact, he has no doubt put this prospect in his forecast with a high probability of closure. (Salespeople and prospects always have a difference of opinion about the probability of a business relationship.)

Hope springs eternal (you wouldn't be in sales if you weren't an optimist) and now the persistent follow up begins. Calls every few days with hopeful voice mail messages are left ("I'm just calling to see if you've made a decision."). Yet the calls are not returned. The call frequency becomes less and eventually the salesperson gives up as he has more hooks out in the stream. The long slow "no" with a free torture treatment is being administered expertly by the prospect. Feeling rejected and inadequate, the salesperson searches for those motivational tapes in his glove box. He'll look for anything to restore his dignity, if only temporarily. Then the whole process repeats itself, again and again.

Summary of the Prospect's Game

Step 1. Hold out the carrot: express interest; possibly withhold information; mislead if necessary.
Step 2. Get educated: pick the salesperson's brain; request a detailed proposal.
Step 3. Avoid commitment: don't be sold; promise to get back to the salesperson.
Step 4. Shop around: evaluate other options; shop the competition.
Step 5. Deflect follow up inquiries: ask for more time to make decision; keep options open.
Step 6. Disappear: disengage from those you won't be doing business with; avoid contact.

What would motivate the prospect to use this system? The answer is simple...a desire to get information and to stay in control.

Summary of the Seller's Traditional Response

Step 1. Find a qualified prospect: find interest level; collect background information; quickly determine needs. (Salespeople typically do a very poor job of investigating needs.)
Step 2. Provide information: pitch features & benefits; demonstrate expertise; attempt to build value and credibility; present a compelling story.

36

Step 3. Ask for the business: handle objections; employ trial closes; handle more objections; negotiate price.

Step 4. Follow up: follow up in a timely and professional manner.

Step 5. Pester: more aggressive and desperate follow up.

Step 6. Disengage: lose interest and experience rejection; look for another opportunity.

Summary of the Traditional Sales Call

Step	Buyer's Process	Seller's Process
1	Hold out the carrot	Find an interested prospect
2	Collect information	Provide information
3	Avoid a commitment	Ask for the business
4	Shop for alternatives	Follow up politely
5	Ask for more time	Pester
6	Disappear	Give up

This scenario creates problems for both parties.

- The buyer is trying to get educated and the salesperson becomes the willing teacher (step 2).
- The salesperson is trying to close the business and the buyer is avoiding a buying decision (step 3).
- The salesperson is following up and being persistent, while the buyer is avoiding contact (steps 4-6).

How can buyers be so skillful at pushing your buttons? A few key statements and questions are all that's needed to get the salesperson to start talking. Have you heard any of these "buying signals" lately?

- "We're thinking about making a change."
- "We've heard good things about your company."
- "We're trying to reduce our costs."
- "Our current supplier hasn't been as responsive as we'd like."

37

- "We've had some problems recently."
- "We'd like to see what other options are available to us."
- "We're looking for better ways to…"
- "We have a problem with….. How would you address that?"
- "Do you think you could help us?"
- "Money's not a problem."
- "I am the decision maker."
- "Can we see a demo?"
- "Can you give us a proposal?"

Clearly the buyer is in control. Let's face it, if you were the salesperson listening to the buyer entice you with these buying signals, would you feel like you had a "live one" (a.k.a. a qualified prospect)? If you didn't have all the business you needed and the buyer asked you for a proposal, how would you respond? Might the phrase, "strike while the iron is hot" be going through your mind? What are the chances you'll go into automatic selling mode when you are asked, "How can you help?"

In the preceding scenarios, the seller's process is totally reactive to the buyer's process. It's been this way since time immemorial. However, it isn't the seller's fault considering that:

- Hope springs eternal; salespeople tend to be optimistic and trusting that the customer will buy.
- Everyone hates rejection, especially salespeople, so they try to avoid hearing "no" at all costs and usually are willing to put up with the buyer's charades.
- Salespeople have been instructed to accept this imbalance as just a normal part of the sales process.
- Salespeople have been told that the more information they present, the higher the likelihood

that the prospect will buy. This has become their core selling philosophy and strategy.

- The pressure to make quotas causes salespeople to ask the wrong questions. They avoid questions that would help them understand the depth and breadth of the prospect's problems, fearing that the problems may not be serious enough to provide a selling opportunity. Instead, they focus on asking questions that help them understand how many dollars to forecast and when the sale might close. This is a huge strategic error. If salespeople fail to understand the prospect's pain they are at a real disadvantage in a complex sale.

We've seen how buyers seduce salespeople into making premature presentations by holding out the proverbial carrot. The process is complicated by an additional dynamic: the misconception that your "special" features and benefits will motivate the prospect to buy from you. In the next chapter we'll explore this issue in a little more depth since it's very important to understand.

Key Points

1. Prospects mislead salespeople; it seems to be genetically encoded.
2. A "think it over" is often just a slow "no" with a free torture treatment.
3. Chances are the prospect's buying process is more effective than your selling process.

Chapter 5
The Traditional Selling Trap

Features and benefits have long been a basic tenet of the selling profession. Features describe a product or service or even tell something about the company. Benefits describe how the feature would help the prospect in some way. For example:

Feature	Benefit
Lifetime warranty	You don't have to worry about product failure
Anti-Lock Braking System	Your car will stop sooner, without skidding; it's safer
Next day delivery	You can get it quickly
24 hour hot line	You'll get answers in a timely manner
Excellent client references	You'll be satisfied with our product or service

You're probably saying, "Well, those are some pretty good reasons for buying. In fact, that'd be my sales pitch, so what's wrong with this approach?" After all, people want to improve their situation in some way, so why wouldn't these be good reasons for making the purchase. Well, they might be great reasons for a transactional sale like buying a car. But, they don't ensure that a good solution has been identified for a business problem.

The following are a few reasons why the feature/benefit approach stalls in a complex relationship based sales opportunity.

- Salespeople use features and benefits prematurely as their sales "pitch," hoping to create interest, instead of properly qualifying the prospect.
- Salespeople mistakenly rely on features and benefits to differentiate themselves from competition, but

everybody's benefits (and often the features) sound the same ("we can save you time and money, and we'll stand behind the purchase 100%"). When competitors look the same, buying decisions are made on price.

- Features and benefits engage the prospect intellectually, and most buying decisions are made emotionally. Research shows that most people don't remember the features or benefits after a week or so, and if they felt any enthusiasm at all, it too had disappeared after a week.
- Features and benefits are the seller's bag of tricks ("we've got this, we've got that"), and may not be relevant to the prospect's buying reasons. People buy for their reasons, not yours.
- Once you've "dumped" your features and benefits, the only thing left to do is close and handle objections and, all too often, discount your price. From there, it's all pressure, and you can't go back and qualify further.

The Playing Field Has Changed

And so have the rules! Selling the way you have in the past no longer gets the results it once did. To continue to do things the same way and expect different results is insanity.

Salespeople must make it their number one priority to become more effective in their selling efforts. After all, it's their profession. Here's a selling system that will put you back in control and help you close a much higher percentage of your proposals with less pressure on both you and the prospective buyer.

Common Sense Selling® – A Sales Process That Works!

CSS is an overall strategy and a set of tactics designed to allow the salesperson an opportunity to maintain control of the sales process without resorting to manipulative measures. This permits parties, buyer and seller, to have a meaningful exchange of information to determine whether or not there is a basis for doing business together.

But, before we can effectively implement a new approach to selling, we have to change some old attitudes regarding the selling process. Without changing our attitudes it will be difficult, if not impossible, to do things differently.

Key Attitudes to Incorporate

- Not everyone is a prospect.
- My time is extremely valuable; my prospect needs to earn my continued involvement in the sales process.
- Hearing a "no" is okay if I've qualified my prospect thoroughly.
- My job is to obtain information, not dispense it.
- My prospect needs to convince me (the salesperson) they have a problem and are serious about solving it.

Key Ingredients for Success

- The focus should be on qualifying, not presenting.
- The right people need to be involved in the process.
- We're not playing games of manipulation any longer.
- Relationship is key and the prospect must trust the salesperson.
- The seller must identify the prospect's "pain" (business issues that need to be resolved).

- The buyer must feel like he made the decision freely and was not pushed into it.

A detailed description of Common Sense Selling® follows in Chapters 7-13.

Key Points
1. Aggressive salespeople create defensive prospects.
2. Old selling techniques don't win long-term clients.
3. People buy for their reasons, not the salesperson's.

Chapter 6
Building Trust and Rapport

Rapport and trust is the foundation for success in sales. The more complex the sale, the higher dollar value of the sale, the more important trust is. Unfortunately, the general perception of salespeople causes buyers to be wary. Initially, the trust factor is very low. The seller starts out at a distinct disadvantage and has an uphill battle. He has to dispel the idea that his primary purpose is to ensnare the buyer.

PRESS HARD, THE THIRD COPY IS YOURS.

Sales resistance is not a natural part of the sales process; it's a direct result of the salesperson's behavior. To eliminate sales resistance, the salesperson must change his behavior.

How Salespeople Destroy Trust

If the salesperson wants to become a valued resource to the buyer, open communication is critical. However, prospects typically do not trust salespeople, feeling uncomfortable, pressured and possibly even threatened. As a result, they resist open communication, preferring to withhold important information so that it cannot be used against them. Salespeople often exacerbate the situation in many unintentional ways, including the following:

- Being late for the appointment
- Making an obviously insincere comment about something in the prospect's office to break the ice
- Being so upbeat and positive that it is obnoxious
- Acting like his product or service is something everybody needs
- Talking too much
- Using a canned presentation
- Using buzz words or jargon that the prospect doesn't understand
- Having a cell phone go off during the meeting
- Presenting a solution before doing a complete diagnosis
- Taking too much time
- Popping surprises, like bringing the boss along without telling the prospect
- Manipulating the prospect by asking leading questions or using other tricky sales moves
- Not being willing to hear "no" from the prospect and pushing too hard for the sale
- In general, simply acting like a salesperson will destroy trust and rapport

Obviously, avoiding the above mistakes will help build trust, but more specifically the salesperson must find a way to remove pressure form the sales interaction. If your prospect thinks that you're there to advance your agenda at his expense, you are in big trouble.

The Trust Quotient

In his best selling book, "The Trusted Advisor," David Maister discusses how trust (the confident expectation of something, according to Webster) is destroyed when the prospect believes you are more interested in making a sale than you are in helping him. While we've taken some liberties with his equation, the message is that the prospect evaluates you in four key areas: rapport, reputation, reliability and your self-interest.

Let's explore this concept because it is very important in building trust with anybody.

Rapport. This is the personal feeling or connection we have with someone; how much we like or dislike them as a person. Factors that influence rapport are:

- Shared experiences
- Being courteous
- Friendliness
- Appearance (dress)
- Matching and mirroring
- Honesty
- Your investigative skills (are you asking the right questions?)
- Impartiality
- Focusing on the prospect
- Degree of sales aggressiveness

Reputation. The external perception that you or your company has in the eyes of others is an important element in determining trust. Reputation can come from:

- Referred by a satisfied client
- Testimonials
- Awards
- Client list
- Memberships
- Personal presence (do you act like you know what you're doing?)

Reliability. The ability to demonstrate to clients whether you are dependable and can be trusted to behave in a consistent manner is also important and can be demonstrated by:

- Showing up on time
- Doing what you say you will do when you said you will do it
- Consistency
- Being prepared
- Returning calls quickly
- Statistics that demonstrate product performance

Obviously, earning as many points as you can in these areas can build trust to a high level. However, all your "credits" can be nullified by what your prospect considers your self-interest, your eagerness to make a sale without regard to the prospect's welfare (and possibly at his expense).

Self-Interest is considered to be high when the salesperson does one or more of the following:

- Appears unwilling to accept a "no" from the prospect
- Pushes too hard to make the sale
- Attempts to manipulate the prospect

- Interrupts the prospect
- Exaggerates
- Does all the talking, pitching their product or service incessantly
- Has a canned answer for every objection
- Suggests some sort of benefit to them (like winning a trip) if the prospect buys
- Appears totally uninterested in problems the prospect wants to fix

If you remember numerators and denominators from 4th grade arithmetic, you'll recall that the equation looks like this:

$$Trust = \frac{Rapport + Reputation + Reliability}{Self - Interest}$$

Do the math! If you can earn 10 points each for rapport, reputation and reliability you have 30 points. If your prospect believes your self-interest is low (as it should be), let's say a 1, you have a trust factor of 30. However, if your prospect thinks your self-interest is high, let's say a 10, then your trust factor is 3. You've lowered your trust factor by 90%! That's a fatal mistake and will cost you the sale every time. Does this help prove the point that it's all about the prospect, not about you?

Connecting With the Prospect

People buy from people they like, and people like people who are like themselves. A few years ago two behavioral scientists, Richard Bandler and John Grinder, developed a concept called NLP (Neuro-Linguistic Programming). This concept recognized that people are most comfortable with people who are similar to them.

Similarity comes in several flavors. Certainly the way we dress is important, since that's what the prospect sees first.   Dress   professionally,   but   for   the   occasion. Increasingly, companies are dressing in "business casual" these days. If you show up in a dark three piece suit, you might look out of place. If you are unsure, err on the side of being slightly overdressed.

The way we communicate is important as well. When we speak of communication, research tells us that the message that people receive from you comes from the words you use, your tonality and your body language. Interestingly, words are the least important, conveying only 7% of the overall message. Tonality (38%) is comprised of three things: the rate of speech (fast or slow), the pitch of our voice (high or low) and the volume (loud or soft). One, I suppose, could add accent or slang to the list, but the experts do not mention this. The last and most important element of communication is body language, which, at 55%, is the most important part of communication. Body language would consist of eye contact, posture, handshake, etc. In other words, 93% of the way we communicate has nothing to do with words. Let's review each category.

Words (7%)

In your communication with prospects, don't talk up (use big words) or down. Use words that are at the same level as those used by your prospect. Don't use slang unless your prospect uses slang and, even then, don't overuse it. Avoid buzzwords and jargon that your prospect may not know or you run the risk of confusing them and making them feel "not okay." Listen for their favorite words and use them unless to do so would come across as too obvious.

Tonality (38%)

You remember when your mother said, "Don't use that tone with me!" Tonality is how we sound when we say the words. Your tone is 3 or 4 times more important than the words that you use. This includes how fast or slowly we speak, how loudly or softly we speak, how high or low our voice is and whether we are animated or speak in a monotone. Think about this. What does a slow speaker think of a fast speaker? *(He's trying to put something over on me.)* What does someone who speaks softly think of someone who speaks loudly? *(What a loudmouth!)* What does someone with a New York accent think of someone with a Southern accent...and vice versa? Our perceptions are heavily influenced by what someone sounds like. It may not be fair, but it happens. People like people who sound like themselves. Be aware of the differences and moderate your behavior accordingly. (Note: This is not manipulation; it is an effort to facilitate communication.)

Body Language (55%)

Body language is the message that you are communicating with your body. It might start with a handshake. Remember the old rule...always have a firm handshake? Well, forget it. What does someone that has a weak handshake think of someone who has a strong handshake? *(Aggressive and overpowering.)*

You communicate with your smile, your posture and your eyes. Eyes are the windows to the soul. Remember the old rule about always having direct eye contact? That too may be misleading. You've met people who never seem to want to "look you in the eye" haven't you? Attempting to draw them into a lot of eye contact may make them uncomfortable. It may be too intense, too intimidating for them.

Posture is another area where people make subconscious judgments about others. Is your prospect sitting back and relaxed or leaning forward and engaged? Is he using his hands a lot or are the hands folded on the desk? Matching his body language conveys the message that "he is like me."

Matching & Mirroring

Consciously communicating with someone in a style that is similar to his or hers is called matching and mirroring. It is a subtle communication expressed through body language, tonality and words. It's not designed to be obvious, but instead a very subtle gesture. Mimicking, or doing exactly what the prospect does, will be perceived as ridiculous and phony. The objective is to create a level of comfort, a feeling of being okay in the situation.

Remember, all things being equal, people do business with people they like, from people who are like themselves.

Salespeople must develop keen interpersonal skills. They must be observant of details and learn to adjust to create a feeling of similarity with their prospect. If your prospect is moving quickly and seems to want to get down to business, what do you think you should do? Would this type of person want to be engaged in small talk about last night's ballgame? Probably not; it would be viewed as useless chatter. If your prospect is friendly and seems to want to talk for a few minutes before getting down to business, what do you think you should do? If you moved right into a presentation in this situation, that could make the prospect feel rushed and make him uncomfortable with you.

Behavioral Styles

People are different in a number of basic ways. Research shows that there are four distinct behavioral or personality styles:

- **Drivers**: Bold and outgoing, fast paced risk takers; they are very businesslike. They focus on the big picture presentations and hate the details. Sometimes called Type A personalities. "Get out of my way" might be their motto.
- **Influencers:** Animated, energetic and friendly, these outgoing people are great talkers but poor listeners. They are optimistic and trusting and relationships are their top priority.
- **Steady Relaters:** Steady relaters are people oriented, but rather reserved. They are very adaptable and are good team players. They dislike risky situations and need to trust you.
- **Cautious Thinkers:** Detail oriented perfectionists; their need to be *right* often slows their decision process down to a crawl. They are skeptical of most salespeople's claims unless backed up by volumes of data. You will usually find them in technical or financial positions.

People with similar profiles find it easy to "connect" with one another. People with dissimilar styles often come away feeling like something was just "wrong," although they may not be able to put their finger on why. Obviously, people don't fit neatly into one of these four categories – there is overlapping. However, most people will have a predominant style.

Can you see the problem when the "driver" salesperson who wants to close quickly runs into an "analytical" buyer who wants to review all the details and take time making a decision? If the salesperson doesn't recognize the problem and adapt, he's in for a frustrating time. How about the super enthusiastic extrovert trying to connect with a reserved buyer? There's going to be a disconnect unless someone adapts his behavior to the other person's style. In sales, it's the salesperson's job to adapt.

Learn what style you are and how you like to sell. Learn to read what your prospect's style is, and how he likes to be sold. If your style is different from his, and you don't adjust, your ability to develop rapport and achieve open and friendly communication probably won't be successful.

Selling is a relationship and problem solving business. You and I are still paying the price for all those sleazy salespeople who created the adversarial atmosphere that exists to this day. Trust is the foundation of any relationship. Here's a concept that may help you keep the balance in your favor.

Assets and Liabilities – The Relationship Balance Sheet

Think of your relationship with a customer or prospect as a balance sheet consisting of assets and liabilities. Some balance sheets are strong - assets exceed liabilities. However, when liabilities exceed assets, the balance sheet is weak and the relationship is in danger.

Every interaction that you have with a customer or prospect creates an impression that is subconsciously filed away as either an asset or a liability. Being on time for an appointment and not overstaying your welcome are assets, although small ones. Being late and overstaying your welcome are liabilities, and can be interpreted by your customer as large ones, depending on the circumstances. Doing a favor or exceeding expectations are big assets; raising prices and missing deadlines are big liabilities. You get the picture.

Take time to evaluate your business relationships. From a balance sheet standpoint, are they strong or weak? Strong relationships can withstand a deposit in the liability column from time to time, while weak ones cannot. Remember the "straw that broke the camel's back"? A weak relationship sometimes is devastated by some seemingly minor problem when, in reality, it was the cumulative effect of many seemingly minor issues that caused the customer to seek other alternatives. Or, you underestimated how important details are to the customer and what might seem like minor missteps to you were perceived as deal breakers to him.

Never take your customer for granted. It's been said that it costs seven times as much to acquire a new customer as it does to do business with an existing one. Do the math.

The Satisfaction Index

A while back we leased a new copier. This machine is just great. It makes color copies, functions as our network printer, has all sorts of neat bells and whistles that have enabled us to do things we never thought possible and the cost per copy is much lower than the last copier we had. On the rare occasion that we need a service call, the tech is here within an hour. Our expectations have not just been met, but completely exceeded.

What happens when you are totally satisfied with a purchase you've made? In our case, we'll gladly provide referrals to the vendor and won't even consider shopping their deal the next time we need a copier.

Satisfaction = Performance - Expectations

Satisfaction is a function of actual performance versus expectations. If you want repeat business and a never-ending supply of referrals, exceed your client's expectations – over-deliver. This is the key to success in business.

Yet all too often salespeople <u>over-promise</u> and under-deliver. They do not exceed their client's expectations – just the opposite. Perhaps they are under pressure to get the business and are willing to exaggerate somewhat to improve the perception of their offering, or maybe they simply have an inflated belief of their product or service's benefits. Whatever the reason, failing to exceed your client's expectations makes your job that much more difficult.

Ask your client what his expectations would be for your product or service if he decided to do business with you. If you can't meet, at the very minimum, or exceed those expectations, you shouldn't do business.

Here are some simple ideas to exceed expectations (and improve your relationship balance sheet):

- Stay in touch
- Handle problems quickly and completely (with a smile)
- Keep them informed, not surprised
- Give them something extra at no charge
- Go the extra mile when you have the opportunity to do so

Making a Great First Impression

Now that you understand the basics, getting off to a good start is critical. What you do when you first meet a new prospect leaves a lasting and important impression. Here are a few areas to focus on:

- **Dress** – appropriately for the occasion.
- **Handshake** – extend your hand to your prospect, but avoid the "bone crusher" handshake. Try to match the prospect's pressure and duration.
- **Eye contact** – direct eye contact is best initially, although you must be aware that some people are

uncomfortable with a lot of direct eye contact and adjust accordingly.

- **Time** – give yourself enough time so that you can arrive about five minutes before the appointment is scheduled. This ensures you will not be late and can relax for a minute or two before the meeting begins.
- **Name** – use the prospect's name when you first meet, but avoid overusing his name. Whether to use Mr. or Ms. instead of first names is a personal thing. Many people today are totally comfortable using first names.
- **Preparation** – do your homework before you arrive. Know something about the company or the person you're meeting. Be ready to compliment them on something they've done recently that is publicly noteworthy or have an intelligent business related question ready.

Rapport is an elusive thing. There are no defined steps to follow to ensure success. Perhaps a good rule to remember is this:

People will forget what you said and they'll forget what you did, but they'll never forget how you made them feel.

Key Points
1. Trust is the foundation of every relationship sale.
2. Minimize your self-interest if you want to maximize trust.
3. People are different. Don't treat everybody the same.

Chapter 7
Why You Need a Selling Process

Some salespeople have a selling system or process - most are just winging it. The sad fact is that studies show that 85% of salespeople are vulnerable to the prospect's machinations because they either do not have a process for selling or their selling process is less effective than their prospect's buying process. As a result, salespeople close at a much lower rate than they should. This makes selling hard work. I'm sure you would agree with this observation.

Why is a selling process important? Simple. Having a selling process improves your results. If you were a contractor building a house, a doctor doing surgery on a patient or a CPA auditing a company's books, you would follow a process, wouldn't you?

A process gives us a step-by-step method to improve quality to ensure the task is completed correctly and expeditiously. In sales, a process creates a common selling language for internal communication and makes it easier for a company to manage the sales function. A process can be taught and replicated.

For you, the salesperson, a process for selling will help you in the following ways:

- More predictable results
- Less pressure on you
- You can identify what went wrong when you did not get the sale
- You can shorten the selling cycle
- You will feel more comfortable when you know what to do next
- A good system that is built on mutual respect, trust and a win/win objective will help you maintain control of the selling process and improve your results

However, not just any process will accomplish your objectives. Your process must be more effective than the prospect's and it must address the manipulative schemes that the prospect sometimes inflicts on you. As mentioned, there is a long history of manipulation and deception on the part of sellers so buyers have looked for ways to gain the upper hand. The level of trust between buyer and seller is, unfortunately, relatively low, even to this day.

But buyers have discovered several things about salespeople. First, salespeople can provide them with information and options that they might not otherwise have. Second, salespeople are normally hungry to make the sale and will do whatever is necessary to play ball with the buyer. Third, salespeople behave in a very predictable way. Based on these observations, buyers have learned how to control the sales process. As discussed in Chapter 4, they mislead you into believing that you have a great opportunity to make a sale, pump you for as much information as they can, stall you when you ask for the business and then disappear. It's a great process that helps them maintain control and get the education that they want. Obviously, you need to have a better process than they do or you'll be held hostage to theirs.

Let's look at the steps of a sales process that has been proven successful in over 150 industries both here in North America and internationally - **Common Sense Selling®**.

Step 1. Opening Meeting Agreement.
The idea is to agree on the timing and the objectives for the meeting and to build trust by letting the prospect know it's okay to say "no." This reduces apprehension and allows the prospect to see the salesperson as a resource, not an adversary. It also helps avoid premature presentations and stalls ("think it overs") and gives the salesperson control of the sales process while the prospect has control over the

content. The Opening Meeting Agreement sets the tone for the meeting…and the relationship.

Step 2. Investigate (Qualify).

Here our goal is to qualify the prospect to determine his or her motivation or "pain," discuss all financial issues including the prospect's willingness to invest in a solution and gain an understanding of the decision-making process. A comprehensive understanding (diagnosis) of all the issues is made. This sets the stage for a targeted solution leading to buyer satisfaction and higher closing rate. It also saves time and eliminates unnecessary proposals that have little chance of being accepted.

Step 3. Closing Plan.

You should test for buying commitment prior to presenting and set up expectations for what will happen when you deliver your proposal. It's important to get a decision when the presentation is made. The "close" actually happens before the presentation since the prospect has been fully qualified and the salesperson will know ahead of time the probability of success. Think of it as "trading" a presentation for a decision.

Step 4. Present Solutions.

The final step is to provide proof your solution will work. Since you have previously discovered, in Step 2, the buyer's selection criteria, budgetary issues and what they need to see to make a decision on your proposal, you will be in a position to offer a targeted solution with all the information they need to say "yes" or "no." Your closing rates will he higher than you ever thought possible. Finally, you will also deal with the possibility of "buyer's remorse" and eliminate competitive retaliation before you leave.

You'll find that although this looks quite simple, it's not. It truly will be a paradigm shift for most of you. Change is uncomfortable, as we've mentioned. You'll find that you are asking far more questions than you ever did. This may take you out of your comfort zone. You will have to fight the tendency to start presenting solutions too soon. However, the final result will be that you will make fewer presentations and close more business. The rewards are there for those willing to change. And there are a lot of changes to be made, as you'll see in the next few chapters.

If you're looking for short-term motivation or a quick fix, you'll be disappointed. There are no shortcuts to becoming a sales leader. Each step in the process must be completed thoroughly or you run the risk of failure. He who does the most thorough job wins. It's that simple!

If you keep doing things the same way you've been doing them, don't expect your results to change.

Key Points
1. Prescription before diagnosis is malpractice in sales as well as medicine.
2. Incorporate an effective selling process and keep it simple.
3. People don't buy features and benefits; they buy solutions to their problems.
4. Solution providers close far more business than product pushers.

Chapter 8
Controlling the Sales Process

Two fundamental problems that we have discussed in previous chapters are that the prospect is typically in control of the sales interaction and there is basic distrust between the buyer and the seller. Unfortunately, the selling environment is often adversarial. This chapter addresses both issues. The person who controls the sales process will go to the playoffs every time. Here we'll discuss one of the most important elements in a relationship sale, the "Meeting Agreement." If you can master meeting agreements you'll be in control of the sales process, reduce the adversarial nature of the relationship and be well on your way to mastering the art of selling.

Remove the Pressure

People hate to be sold, but they love to buy. Buyers hate pressure and the wise salesperson will do everything possible to remove pressure. So, stop selling and let the prospect buy. Here are a few ideas for you to consider to take the pressure off.

Give the prospect the opportunity to say "no" to you. Called an **"Easy Exit"** (see chapters 15-16), it's designed to help the prospect understand that you, the salesperson, realize that not everyone is a prospect, you are comfortable hearing "no," and you won't put any pressure on the prospect to buy. It demonstrates that you understand that the prospect has a right to make a choice. It might sound something like this: "Ms. Prospect, we may get to the end of our meeting today and find out that we really don't have a fit. If that's the case, I want you to understand that I'm okay with your telling me that. I promise I won't try to convince you otherwise if that's your decision." Do you think that might help open up the lines of communication and put the prospect at ease? You bet it will.

Second, stop thinking that your role is to convince people to buy from you. Instead, think that your role is to create an atmosphere where the prospect is comfortable sharing his challenges with you. The ultimate success is when the prospect is convincing you that he has a problem and needs your help. When you adopt this attitude you'll find that your entire approach and demeanor regarding the sales call changes...for the better.

Eliminate Surprises

People hate surprises; dealing with the unexpected causes frustration and pressure. On the contrary, people love to know what to expect. It keeps them feeling relaxed, in charge of the situation. When you implement meeting agreements you'll discover that your prospect will feel more comfortable and relaxed since he knows exactly what to expect when you meet. Without a meeting agreement, you may have a prospect who is wondering how much time the salesperson will take, what exactly will happen during the meeting and be anticipating a strong "close" at the end of the meeting.

Meeting agreements will help eliminate surprises and put the prospect at ease. Here are the basic elements:
1. **Time.** Always establish exactly how much time the prospect will set aside for the meeting. The salesperson should ask, "How much time will we have for our meeting?" The question, as simple as it is, has several purposes. The answer may help you understand the priority level of the prospect's problem (more time will be allotted if the problem is more severe). By allowing the prospect to set the time and duration of the meeting, the prospect will feel more in control. If he feels more in control, that's good for rapport. The number one

complaint about salespeople is that they take too much time from a busy person's schedule. Give the prospects control by allowing them to set the time schedule for the meeting. Once you have agreed on the time for the meeting, it's important that the salesperson respect the time allotted.

2. **Prospect's Agenda.** It's important to determine what they want to accomplish by meeting with you. Ask a simple question like, "From your perspective, what's important for us to cover during our meeting?" This stimulates communication and helps you zero in on the prospect's critical business issues so you can determine whether you can offer a viable solution. Their answer often tells you whether they are looking for solutions to problems or just collecting information.

3. **Salesperson's Purpose**. The second part of the agenda concerns what is important to the salesperson during the meeting. In an initial meeting it's important for the salesperson to get permission to ask questions so that a thorough diagnosis can be made. This might sound like, "When we get together, I would like to ask some questions to get a better understanding of the issues that you're facing. Is that okay?" Giving you permission to ask questions gives the prospect a feeling of control and sets the stage for an exchange of information as opposed to an information dump by the salesperson.

4. **Next Step.** The final part of the meeting agreement is to agree to reach a decision whether or not to move forward at the end of the meeting. We want to tell the prospect before our meeting that he should be comfortable telling us if he is not interested. If his answer is "no," that's okay. There's always the chance that our company and our potential solutions may not be an appropriate fit for his business challenges. On the other hand, if the prospect has interest in talking further, we'd want to agree on what our next steps would be. When we give someone the right to choose,

it gives them control over the outcome and is great for building rapport and trust.

SALES PROS ARE CAREFUL TO
ELIMINATE PRESSURE, NOT CREATE IT.

Benefits of the Meeting Agreement

Any sales 'technique" that puts the buyer at a disadvantage is inappropriate. Meeting agreements are good for both the buyer and the seller, as you'll see.

- Control is important for both parties. Meeting agreements allow the seller to control the sales process while giving the prospect control of the content (time, agenda and the ability to say "no") of the call.
- We ensure that we have enough time to have an effective meeting.
- Both parties are on the same page with respect to what they are trying to accomplish.
- The salesperson has permission to ask questions and the prospect understands that working

collaboratively to determine if there is a solution is an important part of the meeting.

- The prospect will feel more at ease with the salesperson and will be inclined to provide more information since he knows that the salesperson is comfortable hearing "no." (Interestingly, the more opportunities you give the prospect to tell you "no," the fewer "no's" you will hear.)
- There is agreement at the end of the meeting as to what will happen next. The often-heard response, "I need to think it over," is eliminated.
- If, at the end of the meeting, it's apparent that there is no point in continuing to talk, we can close the file and move on.

Several years ago the sales manager of a local company told us that although his sales numbers were below expectations, his salespeople were very experienced and the only help that they needed would be in the areas of time management and effective follow up. He explained that they had a lot of proposals on the street and were "working overtime" following up with their prospects. He suggested that they needed better "techniques" to get these prospects to return their calls. When we asked him what his closing rate was, he admitted that it was about 15%.

His people were in the "proposal mill" business. They gave proposals to everybody. Their selling philosophy was the more proposals you have on the street, the more business you'll get. That's old thinking, yet for many salespeople it's their primary selling strategy. We're not saying it doesn't work, sometimes it's just not very effective. No wonder they were working overtime. They spent most of their time chasing leads and writing proposals that had little hope of successful outcomes.

The sales manager didn't get it. His team needed a complete makeover and although it took him a while to realize it, his problems were not in the area of time management and following up. They were in the area of qualifying. They had no concept of qualifying prospects; asking questions was unfamiliar territory. They were product pitchmen, pure and simple, and they were struggling, big time.

When we finished training, his group understood how to uncover the prospect's business issues and whether or not they should invest time with the prospect. They learned that not everybody qualifies for a proposal and how to differentiate suspects from real prospects. Their time management problems disappeared because they didn't have to waste tons of time "following up." They had more time for prospecting and they felt better about themselves because they were no longer pestering people who really didn't want to hear from them.

Qualifying is the most important skill that a sales professional can possess. The companies that we've trained seem to agree that one of the major benefits of using Common Sense Selling© is that they qualify more effectively and spend far less time with prospects who probably would never have bought from them. How to become a great investigator will be the focus for the next few chapters of the book.

Key Points

1. Use meeting agreements to take control of the sales process and set the tone for a relationship that is built on trust, regardless of the outcome.
2. Tell the prospect that you are comfortable hearing "no" if there is not a good fit between your companies.

Chapter 9
Discovering the Buyer's Motivation

In our sales seminars we ask participants if they think salespeople qualify adequately. The answer is, unanimously, "no." It's a self-indictment, but it's true. Unfortunately, the majority of salespeople do a very poor job of qualifying. Studies show that too many assumptions are made with regard to what the prospect's problems are, how severe they might be and how eager the prospect is to find and implement a solution. Salespeople seem to have a "one size fits all" mentality. All of this leads to a premature presentation and, ultimately, failure.

Think of an iceberg. About 10% is above water. It's the obvious part, but not the most important. Typically salespeople see the tip of the iceberg and think they understand what's beneath the water's surface. If the iceberg represents the prospect's pain, then most of it is hidden beneath the surface. And the hidden part is the most important. Too many assumptions are made.

Salespeople must be able to fully understand the prospect's pain. Pain is the difference between what they have and what they want; their present situation versus their desired situation; their unresolved business issues. There are two classifications under the term "pain:" pain (things are bad and need fixing) or gain (things are good, but could be considerably better). Pain is what motivates the prospect to take action. (We'll use the term pain exclusively in this book.) Salespeople need to know the following:

- Does the prospect's motivation come from a problem that needs to be addressed today (pain), a problem that might arise in the future (fear), or simply an interest in getting more information (curiosity)? (People spend more money, faster, to fix pain.   They don't invest much to satisfy curiosity.)

- What are the causes of the pain?
- What problems (business and personal) has the pain created?
- How committed is the prospect to taking action to fix the problem?
- What would an ideal resolution be?

It's important to come armed with a good list of questions that will uncover this information and the means to maintain control of the conversation to keep the prospect talking during this "discovery" process.

Qualifying for motivation or pain is time consuming, but it is the most important thing a salesperson can do. And, because the prospect wants to guard against appearing too vulnerable to you, it's important to remove any and all pressure from the sales conversation. A good tactic to do this is to tell him/her up front that it's okay to tell you "no" if there's not a fit.

Discovering the prospect's pain is a process. It's a series of questions that takes the prospect from an intellectual, big picture level to an emotional level describing personal consequences and commitment. Here are the types of questions that will help you become a world-class qualifier.

Background Questions. You'll need to find out various facts about the prospect's situation that relate to your product or service. They are not usually "pain" related, but are relevant to the business relationship that you are trying to develop. They typically are descriptive of the prospect's current situation and can begin to give you an understanding of the scope of the opportunity. They can include things like:

- How many users are on the system.

- Who their current supplier is and how long they have used them.
- What their current process is.
- Where their locations are.
- Etc.

However, you must do your homework ahead of time to determine appropriate, useful questions. Prospects do not want to take the time to educate you about their business.

Pain Symptom Questions. Remember the definition of pain (or gain)? It's the difference between where they are (what they have) today and where they want to be (what they want to have) tomorrow. These questions uncover the tip of the pain iceberg.

You might try a few of these questions to get the prospect to start telling you about surface pain:
- "What are the mains concerns you're having with respect to.....?"
- "What challenges are you facing that a company like mine might be able to help you with?"
- "Usually people come to us for help in one or more of the following areas (list 2-3 problems you solve for people); are any of these issues for you?"

When you ask questions like this, look for the prospect to make statements like:
- "My sales are not where I want them to be."
- "Our current supplier is having problems with....."
- "We're having trouble processing all this paperwork efficiently."
- "I don't think I'll be able to maintain my current lifestyle when I retire."
- "Our system crashes frequently."
- "We're spending too much on....."
- "We're not happy with....."

Cause Questions. Look for the reasons for the pain. What's causing the disparity? Typically there are several causes for the pain. Pay close attention as these are the issues you will ultimately try to resolve for the prospect. This information leads you to your presentation.

Here are some ideas for questions that will help you understand the depth and breadth of the problems:

- "What are the reasons this is going on?"
- "Why do you suppose this is happening?"
- "Do you know what's causing these problems?"

It's vital for you to understand - even better than the prospect – what's causing the pain. You'll hear things like:

- "We're not in front of enough prospects and waste too much time with unqualified prospects."
- "Our current supplier is having quality and delivery problems."
- "We don't have the right software and our people need training."
- "I haven't been able to put away enough money and our investments aren't getting us the kind of return we had hoped for."
- "The server is overloaded."

Consequence or Impact Questions. Elicit from the prospect the impact that the overall pain has on the company (or the family) and the individuals involved. Understanding the consequences motivates the prospect to take action.

Ask questions such as these to discover the consequences:

- "What kinds of problems is this causing for you?"
- "How is it impacting the company?"
- "What is it costing the company?"
- "How long has it been a problem?"
- "How is it impacting you personally?"

- "What impact is it having on sales and profitability?"
- "Seems like this might affect....., does it? Can you tell me more?"
- "What happens if it doesn't get fixed?"
- "Who else cares about it?"

YOUR CREDIBILITY COMES FROM YOUR QUESTIONS, NOT FROM YOUR SALES PITCH.

They'll say things like:
- "I'm under a lot of pressure to turn sales around and we're having to offer discounts to move product. Our margins are down by 20%."
- "It's affecting our ability to meet our customers' expectations. We're starting to lose business."

- "Our reports are not timely and the information is suspect. We've had to delay an important product launch and it's costing us thousands."
- "I'll have to work longer than I planned and we won't be able to travel like we wanted when I retire."
- "I'm getting calls on weekends and working all kinds of hours. It's affecting my home life."

Resolution Questions. If you ask, the prospect will tell you how they'd like the problem to be resolved; what their vision is for a solution. This is a key point. A complete qualifying process must discover what the prospect wants as a result of his contact with you.

These questions will help you find what the prospect's vision is:

- "What are you currently doing to address these issues?"
- "How are those solutions working out?"
- "What would a perfect solution look like?"
- "What kind of help are you looking for?"
- "What are you hoping we could do?"

And the answers might sound like:

- "We tried ...., but the results were disappointing."
- "It's critical that we implement a training program that will ....."
- "We've got to find a supplier that can....."
- "We've got to find a solution that will..... within the next 90 days."
- "We've got to find a way to reduce our tax burden and save at least another $1000 a month soon."
- "We need a new server in the next 90 days."

Commitment Questions. Commitment questions help determine how important it is to rectify the situation and what action the prospect might take if you were able to provide a solution that they felt would work. Although they might have a problem, it's wrong to assume they are committed or have a budget to fix it.

Ask questions like these to see how strong their commitment is:

- "How important is it to fix this problem?"
- "What priority is it to fix this problem?"
- "Is doing nothing an option?"
- "You've probably got a lot of things you have to deal with. What priority would you say this is?"
- "Assuming we could take care of the problem, what would happen at that point?"

How will you feel when your prospect starts to say things like this?

- "We'd want to get started as soon as possible."
- "We'd be willing to start switching some of our business over by (date) if we felt you could do the job."
- "We'd get started right away if we thought it would work."
- "I'd write a PO now if I knew it would solve the problem."
- "How soon could you get started if we approve the plans?"

Keep Your Prospect Talking

Learn to direct the conversation and keep the prospect talking. When he is talking he's giving you valuable information. When you're monopolizing the conversation you're losing an opportunity to discover what will motivate him to take action. Add these types of questions to your repertoire and you'll gain a deeper understanding of the issues.

- "Tell me more about that."
- "What else is there?"
- "Can you elaborate on that?"
- "How does that impact your ability to…..?"
- "Is there anything else?"
- "Could you be a little more specific?"
- "What else do I need to know about that?"

The ability to qualify the prospect and understand his pain is one of the most important jobs the salesperson has. Once you learn how to qualify the prospect, you will close a much higher percentage of your proposals. And, you will be providing valuable solutions and gaining referrals.

The Top Ten Tips for Finding Pain
1. The prospect must convince you that there's a problem and that it's important to find a solution.
2. People don't buy features and the related benefits, they buy solutions to their problems.
3. People buy emotionally and justify their decisions logically.
4. Prescription before diagnosis is malpractice.
5. No pain, no change.
6. Features and benefits used prematurely are the primary cause of the prospect's objections.
7. Observe the 70/30 rule when qualifying your prospect. Let him do most of the talking.
8. You get your credibility by the type of qualifying questions you ask, not by the length and enthusiasm of your sales pitch.
9. The more effective you are at qualifying, the easier the close will be.
10. If you say it, they can doubt it; if they say it, they believe it.

74

Key Points
1. The best investigators are the best closers.
2. Qualifying is the most important thing a salesperson can do.
3. Become a great qualifier and close more business, faster.

Chapter 10
"Show Me the Money"

Understanding the financial details relative to the sale is critical. You must take the time to discover the following:

- The financial impact of the pain on the company and the prospect
- What the prospect is willing to invest to eliminate the pain
- The financial resources available to address the pain

Interestingly, most salespeople seem uncomfortable discussing money and do a relatively poor job in this critical area. Here are the major reasons.

Many of us think that talking about money is impolite. When I was about nine or ten, I remember asking my mother how much money my dad made. To this day I recall her response. "It's really not polite to ask questions like that." And to this day I'm sensitive about discussing financial issues with people. So I have to get out of my comfort zone when discussing budget issues with prospects. Often our self-limiting beliefs can create success barriers in sales. The money issue is a good example. Think about it. When your neighbors come home with a new car and you're in their driveway admiring it, how comfortable are you asking them what they paid for it? You might ask if they got a good deal, but usually that's the end of it. Many of us struggle with discussions about money.

Another self-limiting belief that some of us have about money revolves around what really constitutes "a lot of" money. If you're asking someone to invest $2,000 to buy your product or service and that $2,000 represents a lot of money to you, it might be difficult for you to pull the trigger and ask for it. If the prospect said, "that's quite a bit of money, I'd need some time to think it over," that would be a put off that you might accept as being reasonable. The same thought might be going through your mind. It's called buyer's empathy; you can absolutely understand and relate to how the buyer feels.

A third reason that salespeople don't like to discuss money is that they are afraid the prospect might not have the budget to make a purchase. They avoid talking about money and hope that a compelling presentation will overcome any money objections. This is a huge strategic error.

Finally, salespeople don't discuss money because they believe they can "create value" by telling a prospect how great their product is. This is a critical mistake. Remember, telling isn't selling!

The consequences of having an incomplete understanding of the financial issues are serious. First, the prospect may not be able to afford your solution and may reject your proposal. Second, the pain may not be compelling enough to warrant an investment. Third, your proposal may be inadequate to resolve their pain. All will seriously impede your ability to get the business.

How To Discuss Money Issues

First, don't talk about your price or their budget until you've uncovered their pain. Talking about money prematurely will cause the focus of the discussion to be price related and you'll get more price objections than you want. If you discuss money too early, before you have been able to build value by determining what the pain is costing, your price will often be seen as excessive.

There is an inverse relationship between the magnitude of the problem (or opportunity) and the money the prospect will spend to fix it. The more pain they have, the less the financial investment is an issue. It's vital to take the time to uncover the financial impact of the pain or the anticipated financial impact of the opportunity in your initial qualifying efforts.

This area is critically important in a complex sale where you are selling expensive solutions. By doing a complete diagnosis and determining the cost of each pain, you are able to start building value for your eventual solution.

It is important to discuss, in general terms, what a solution would cost and what the prospect would receive for that investment prior to your presentation, proposal or demo. If you wait until afterward, two things may happen:

1. Your prospect won't be able to pay close attention to your proposal because he's wondering what it's going to cost.
2. If you and your company have invested significant financial resources to do the demo or proposal, you are in a more difficult negotiating position. (The thinking is, "We've got a lot invested in this deal and we don't want to lose it.")

As a general rule both you and your prospect should be on the same page with respect to what the problem's approximate financial impact is and how much your solution might cost before you agree to make a formal presentation.

You should get a general expectation of what they would spend to address the issues and find out if that money is actually available. You also have to determine if they'd be willing to invest it if you had the right solution.

Financial Questions

Here are a few very effective questions that will uncover the financial issues associated with many selling opportunities. This is another opportunity to make up some 3 X 5 cards to help you commit the questions to memory.

- "Do you have a budget to take care of the problem? What would it be, approximately?"
- "What kind of resources has the company committed to fix the problem?"
- "Is there a financial impact? How much would you guess, in round numbers?"
- "Can you put a finger on what the problem is costing you? Is that a lot of money for your company?"
- "How much is that costing you annually? If you were able to recoup those dollars because of what we did for you, how much would drop to the bottom line?"
- "Would you be willing to invest a minimum of_____ (between___ and ___) to fix it?"
- "If it cost _____ , would you be willing to make that kind of investment?"
- "Assuming we could make the problem go away, how much would you be willing to invest to fix a $_____ problem?"
- "If you came to believe we could fix it and it would cost $ _____, would that money be available?"

Key Points
1. Budget must be addressed after the pain is uncovered, not before, since premature budget discussions tend to create early price resistance.
2. The prospect needs to convince the salesperson they would be willing to spend the money if they had the conviction the solution would work.
3. If the prospect doesn't have adequate budget or isn't willing to make the investment, you don't have a very good prospect.

Chapter 11
Understanding the Decision Process

Several years ago we were training a group of high tech salespeople from a large company in Silicon Valley. As we began to discuss how to understand the prospect's decision process, the EVP of World Wide Sales inconspicuously entered from the back of the room and sat down. A minute or two later, one of the salespeople asked us, "How do you move yourself up the ladder in a company so you can get to talk to the decision maker?"

A loud "explosion" came from the back of the room, startling everyone. It was the EVP who shouted, "That's the biggest problem we have around here. You guys start too low. You've got to start at the top! That's what separates the great salespeople from the average ones!" Then he walked out of the room. Everyone received his message loud and clear. And he was absolutely correct.

Over half the problems encountered by salespeople are caused by their inability to gain access to the decision maker. When we provide coaching to our clients on selling challenges they are experiencing with their prospects, it's clear that many of their challenges are due to the fact that they do not have access to the decision maker. Failure to be in front of the person with the ultimate authority to approve the purchase will, in every case, eliminate your ability to get a positive decision. You will, however, get lots of stalls ("I need to run it by...") and plenty of "think it overs."

Since one of your biggest challenges is to gain access to the decision maker, let's take a moment to look at some proven tactics that will help you accomplish this difficult task and help you avoid spending your time with the wrong people.

Tactics for Gaining Access to the Decision Maker

Unfortunately, besides asking, "Who makes the final decision?," or words to that effect, most salespeople aren't very creative when it comes to gaining access to the decision maker. Here are a few, hopefully novel, ideas that will improve your chances .

- **First and foremost, start at the top.** You've got to be in front of the decision maker. That's the only rule that counts. Everything else is starting from a position of weakness. Here are some other ideas to get you there and keep you there.

- **Assume it.** Early in the sales call ask, "When am I meeting with the decision maker?" If you get some push back, you need to say, "I'm confused; why not?"

- **Ask for it.** Simply state, "I'll need to meet with the decision maker. Can you arrange the meeting?" (I'm confused; why not?)

- **Tell them.** "In order to completely understand the issues from everyone's point of view, the decision maker will need to be a part of this from the start." This is not posturing; it's true, and it's important.

- **"Company policy."** "It's company policy that we meet with the decision maker." (Maybe it isn't, but maybe it should be.)

- **Bargain for access.** Some lower level folks who want to protect their "turf" or have an ego trip may deny you access until you've "proven" yourself. In cases like this it's important to find out under what circumstances they would introduce you to the decision maker. When you've found that out simply state, "So if I understand this correctly, in return for proving to you that we can adequately address your challenges, you will introduce me to the decision maker. Right?"

- **Justification.** "I need to understand the issues from everyone's point of view. If I don't understand what the decision maker's issues are, my proposal may miss the mark. That's probably not a good strategy for either of us, is it?"

- **"Biggest concern."** "My biggest concern is that I won't be able to meet with the decision maker during this process and that might impact my ability to completely understand the company's challenges and ultimately present a really good solution. Can we avoid that?"

- **Peer to peer.** "Our president (EVP) wants to come to the meeting and wants to meet your president. Sorry, I have no control over this. Will you let the him know?" Obviously this tactic gets other people involved, but sometimes that's important.

- **Surrogate authority.** "I understand that the decision maker won't be available for my presentation. Here's what I'd like to do. Tell me if it's okay with you. I'll make my presentation to you. If it was your decision, tell me what you'd say. If you wouldn't want to go forward, just tell me that. I'm okay with a no. But if you felt it was the best solution, what would happen then (or would you feel comfortable recommending it to the decision maker)?"

- **Asking for help.** People want to help other people. Use comments like, "I've got a problem and I need your help" or "I'm a little confused." You'll be surprised at how much mileage you get from this tactic.

- **Fly on the wall.** Use this tactic when the decision is made by a committee or some other group of individuals behind closed doors. Say something like the following. "My biggest concern is that during the meeting the committee members will start asking you questions that you don't have answers to. That might make you feel uncomfortable and it might cause the whole thing to get tabled or, worse, shot down. I really don't want that to happen to you. We could avoid that by letting me be present for your presentation. You do the talking and I'll just be there to answer any difficult questions that come up. Think we could do that?"

You can embellish this tactic with a third party story. "Just last month I ran into a situation similar to this. The committee was making the decision and my contact was making the pitch for me. They asked him some questions that he couldn't answer and the whole thing went south in a hurry. And worse, my guy was really put on the spot and felt stupid because he couldn't answer their questions. I wouldn't want that to happen to you."

- **Hangin' around the lobby.** This is similar to the fly on the wall, but you suggest that you just "hang out" in the lobby (or being available by phone) while they're having the meeting. If you're needed, they can ask you to come in to answer a question or provide some clarification, then leave the meeting. (Once you're in they'll probably let you stay.) Your competitors probably aren't volunteering to do this, so your higher level of interest in doing business with them might just give you a slight edge.

Often we are successful in starting at the top, but get "sent down" in the organization by the decision maker who wants to delegate all or some of the responsibility to a subordinate. If so, don't lose your ability to stay in touch with the decision maker. Tell him you'd be happy to talk to the subordinate, but before you leave find out the following:

- Find out what pains he (the decision maker) has and what his ideal solution would be.
- Ask what authority the subordinate has to make the decision.
- Find out if money is available and if the subordinate can spend it.
- Ask who else might have important input into the final decision.
- Ask the decision maker if you can touch bases from time to time to keep him informed of your progress or how he would like you to stay in touch throughout the process.

Remember the problems we discussed in qualifying fully for money issues? All too often we have the same problems understanding the decision process. Here's why.

- We're not sure what information we're supposed to find out.
- We take shortcuts because it's easy.
- We actually believe the decision maker is inaccessible.
- We're afraid we'll insult someone by suggesting he may not have the authority to make a decision.
- Trust and optimism are two character traits shared by the majority of salespeople, so we trust the subordinate to sell it for us.
- We're comfortable with a low closing percentage like 20%.

Five Key Areas of Decision Qualification

The Players. We need to understand where the authority for the final decision rests and what role the subordinates (influencers) play, and we need to conduct our sales efforts

84

primarily with the decision maker, not the subordinates. Attempting to secure the business by working with people without real authority is a poor strategy, leading to extended sales cycles and low closing rates.

Our experience shows that salespeople typically call one or two levels too low in the organization. There are numerous reasons why this happens. First and foremost, it's easier to get an appointment with a lower level person. They are the information gatherers and are only too happy for you to come in and educate them. Some, however, actually get power from blocking you from the real decision authority.

Second, salespeople are constantly being pressured by their sales managers to make more appointments, so pretty soon they're meeting with anyone who will talk to them. They rationalize that they can work their way up in the organization, but it rarely happens.

Remember the self-limiting beliefs we discussed earlier? If the little voice in your head tells you that you shouldn't bother important people (they're too busy to see me, I'm just a salesperson, etc.), what's going through your head when you try to call the company president or other top official? You've got it... anxiety, hesitation and a rush back to the comfort zone of calling on a lower level influencer.

It's important to understand that people who don't have the authority to make decisions can't say yes (but they can say no), and they're not very effective at selling your solutions to their superiors, certainly not as good as you would be. And because they are not at the highest levels, they often don't even know the real issues the company is trying to rectify. You'll easily double your closing rate by working harder to get yourself in front of the right people.

While we stress the importance of having clear and frequent access to the decision maker, others in the organization can play an important part in the decision process. Take the time to meet them and find out what their pains are and what part they will play. Find out who might be a champion for your competition and try to build your case with them. The more complex the sale, the more important these people become. Don't overlook their importance.

Timetable. When will the prospect make a decision? Their timetable often provides clues as to the severity of their pain and how they prioritize this business challenge. Their timing also will help you understand how to manage your time for this opportunity. Optimally, you will work within the prospect's timetable and bring your solution to them at exactly the time when they are ready for it.

Decision Criteria. What criteria will they use to make a decision? This is not an area to make assumptions based on your experience. The decision criteria are different for every prospect. Certainly there is often some commonality, but the professional salesperson will have the prospect explain these criteria and rank them from most to least important. Understanding their criteria is critical when dealing with competition.

Typically buying criteria are directly related to pain. For example, if the prospect's principle pain issues are in the area of service, their number one buying criteria will revolve around your ability to improve their service. Price will be secondary. By the same token, if you have failed to uncover serious pain issues, expect the primary criteria for making a change to be price related and you'll be fighting off the price objections.

It is your responsibility to stop the process if the prospect identifies one or more buying criteria that you cannot satisfy. You might have to say, "I'm sorry, our product can't do that. Is that a deal breaker?" If it is and you have to abort, you've saved yourself and the prospect valuable time. Plus, you've gained the prospect's respect since you didn't attempt to force a solution where it was not appropriate.

Here's the bottom line – with respect to selection criteria, the more pain you are able to uncover, the less important price will be in their decision process.

Proposal Content. This is another area where assumptions can hurt you, since people evaluate things differently. When you present a proposal, your objective should be to give the prospect the exact information that he needs to make a "yes" or "no" decision – no more and no less. This approach greatly improves your chances of securing the business.

In one of the largest training programs we ever completed, with a 6,000 person sales force, we asked the MAN what he needed to see from us so he could make a decision when we delivered the proposal. We were expecting to hear, "I want a detailed proposal with an execution plan, testimonials, financial history of your company, etc." Instead, all he wanted was one page with just the bullet points and a place to sign. Had we not asked, we would have wasted hours putting together a detailed proposal that would have bored him stiff. He got what he wanted, no more and no less, and engaged us on the spot.

Roadblocks. Try to determine what roadblocks might be encountered that would delay implementation of the solution. Did you ever run into a situation where the purchasing department wanted to negotiate a lower price or get competitive bids after the VP generated a purchase order for your product? Asking this question may uncover some issues that previously had not come to light, such as other decision makers or budget issues. Checking for roadblocks helps to ensure that qualification is complete and eliminates surprises.

Asking about roadblocks will also make your prospect think. We posed this question to the VP of Sales for a large magazine publisher that had a division that sold market research. Her answer was surprising. She said that her division was being sold and that she really wanted to get some training for her group before the sale was completed. She said she would walk the PO through immediately before everything got put on hold. That one question probably saved the training program for us.

Decision Process Questions

How well do you understand your prospect's decision-making process? Read through the following questions and find a few that fit your circumstances and style. Try them on your next sales call and see how much more information you'll get.

- "What process will you go through to make the decision?"
- "How does your company go about making a decision to invest $ _____ to fix a problem like this?"
- "What info do you need to make a decision?"
- "Isn't it safe to say that before you make a decision you're going to need to be comfortable with a number of things. Would you share those with me?"
- "Whose opinion (if anyone's) would you get to help you make the decision?"
- "Will you get help from anyone to make the decision?"
- "Once you've made the decision, what bureaucracy do you have to go through to get it implemented?"
- "Does anyone else have to agree?"
- "How would you know that we're the company that could help you?"
- "Are there any special concerns that need to be addressed before we could work together?"

- "What criteria would you use to make the decision? Which is most important?"
- "What conditions would have to be present for us to do business together?"
- "What sequence of events would need to take place for this to happen?"
- "What roadblocks could stop the process?"
- "What do you need to develop the conviction that I can help you fix _____?"

As previously mentioned, the Common Sense Selling® approach requires a paradigm shift. There's a lot to remember. But you'll improve your chances of success if you just remember not to make a presentation to anyone who can't, or won't, make a decision.

Key Points
1. Get to know the cast of characters.
2. Try to cultivate a coach or internal advocate who can help you navigate through the landmines.
3. Don't make a presentation to anyone who can't or won't make a decision.

Chapter 12
How To Triple Your
Proposal Success Rate

I don't like the term "closing," but it's a fact of life in sales. The negative connotations are everywhere – people hate to be "closed," and rightfully associate closing with pressure and manipulation. It's given selling a bad name.

Closing in a complex sale is a different animal, however. Pressure and manipulation are anathema, destroying trust and rapport, elements critical to success in a complex sale.

I've been selling and studying selling for a very long time and I've always been frustrated at the lack of information about closing in the complex sale. There's certainly been volumes written on closing in simple, transactional sale; virtually all of it of the manipulative, hard sell variety, as previously mentioned. The ABC approach (Always Be Closing), made famous by the "Glengarry, Glen Ross" movie, comes immediately to mind.

In a complex sale, most of the advice on closing sounds like this:

- Closing is the natural result of two people who want to work together, and
- Don't forget to ask for the order.

Okay, not bad advice, but there's not much substance there, unfortunately. With the average closing rate for salespeople in the 20-25% range, a strong argument can be made that there needs to be more solid advice on how to improve closing rates. Typically, four proposals out of five are unsuccessful; a pathetic (and costly) success rate by anybody's standards. And the failures are very time consuming. Most often several meetings are required with the prospective client, followed by a preliminary term sheet, then preparation and delivery of the proposal, negotiation, follow up, etc. The entire process often takes months – a significant time investment for everybody. Failure to win the business at the end of the process is very costly. To use a baseball analogy, an abysmal .200 batting average won't get you into the pro ranks; why should it be acceptable in selling?

There's no reason why you shouldn't be successful 70-80% of the time. It is eminently do-able, as proven by the very best professional salespeople.

Our analysis and research indicates that closing in a complex sale seems to boil down to several simple procedures: doing a lot of things right over the entire sales cycle with the prospect; always knowing exactly what will happen next; knowing when to get out and cut your losses; and satisfying the needs of your client. Basically, it's all about eliminating the factors that contribute to a failed effort.

Let's take a closer (no pun intended) look at how you can win three out of every four deals you decide to pursue, how you can exceed your sales quota every time, and ultimately, make as much money as you want.

The three keys to being a 75% closer are execution, elimination and delivery.

1. Execution

It's not what you do <u>when</u> you close, it's what you do <u>before</u> you close that matters. Executing the basics of Common Sense Selling© flawlessly will help put you in the driver's seat to win the business. These principles have been covered in great detail in the previous chapters, but as a review and to reinforce the concepts, you must focus on the following:

- Building trust and rapport. People won't give you the opportunity to help them solve a major business or personal challenge unless they trust you. And that trust comes from your demonstrating interest in helping them solve a problem, not from your interest in simply selling them something.
- Qualify completely. This includes understanding their challenges (pain) as well as they do, making absolutely sure they've got the resources to fix the problem, and understanding all the elements of their decision process. You must determine why they'd be willing to leave the incumbent and do establish a business relationship with you. And throughout it all, it's critical to maintain control of the sales process.
- Follow the CSS process and the process will make you successful. Every shortcut you take will reduce your chance of success.

2. Elimination

Perhaps as many as 50% of the proposals that salespeople make have virtually no chance of success. Most salespeople will offer a proposal to virtually any prospect if asked; they just can't seem to say "no." If you pay attention to the warning signs (yes, there are very clear warning signs), you can save yourself a great deal of time and frustration. You can give yourself plenty of extra time to pursue prospects that are a better fit, that offer a higher probability of success.

If you honestly reflect on some of the "opportunities" you've worked on in the past, you'd probably agree that more than a few were complete efforts in futility, but you pursued them in spite of the fact that you suspected you had little or no chance of winning the business. In hindsight you probably wished you'd never gotten involved. So why did you? Why didn't you simply pass?

Maybe you couldn't disengage because your pipeline was empty. Maybe you chose to overlook the obvious in the hope that you'd be successful. Perhaps you are measured by the number of proposals you have on the street. Or maybe your manager put pressure on you to go for it because the company needed the "business." Whatever the reason, it didn't change the outcome – lots of time and money invested for zero return.

Those days can be over, but you've got to make some changes. I can show you how to fix the problem – how to close more of the proposals that you make and how to fix your time management problem and give yourself more quality selling time. Follow this advice and you'll be selling more with less effort. One of the secrets is to select only those opportunities that offer you the best chance to be successful, and that's relatively easy if you know what to look for.

Early Warning Signs

Think of every opportunity as having a set of traffic signals to guide you. Green light means go, yellow means proceed with caution, and red indicates STOP. Follow the lights and you'll be able to weed out dead deals faster, give yourself far more time to pursue opportunities you have a good chance of winning, and drastically reduce the wear and tear on your ego by striking out fewer times.

The first warning signs present themselves quickly, and that's a great advantage for you. Every prospect must pass this first qualifying hurdle, or you must disengage quickly.

We've all met prospects who have been somewhat antagonistic, unwilling to talk, or vague in their answers to our questions. They give you the impression that they'd prefer to be doing something else other than meeting with you. These folks are not good prospects. But salespeople, despite the obvious danger signals, are almost completely reluctant to disengage. The "hope-a-hope-a" strategy is firmly entrenched, along with a liberal dose of denial of the obvious warning signs. This old adage comes to mind...if it walks like a duck and quacks like a duck, it probably IS a duck. Well, if it exhibits all the initial early warning signs of a bad prospect, it probably IS a bad prospect.

The good ones deserve your time and effort. The rest should be dumped like a bad habit. There are four initial qualifiers that, if answered negatively or in a vague manner, are strong indicators that your continued efforts with the prospect may not be worthwhile. Here they are...

- Is the prospect friendly? (If he's not, you can bet he's probably pretty happy with his current supplier, and may just be shopping you.)
- Will the prospect answer your questions? (Open communication is a key to any good business relationship; why waste time with someone who won't open up with you?)
- Does the prospect know what he wants? (If he doesn't know what he wants, how can you satisfy his needs?)
- Does he want it in a relatively short time frame? (Most likely you need the business now; if they don't need a solution now, their problem probably isn't very serious.)

You should be able to determine these things in the first meeting with a prospect; perhaps even during the first phone call.

If you're getting a bunch of negative answers to the above, it is probably time to say "Adios" and move on. Here's a professional way to bow out:

> "Based on what you've said, I don't think we'll be able to help you. Generally the folks we work with have a very clear understanding of what they want

and are in the market for it now. Would you like me to suggest a company that might be able to help you?" (Think about suggesting a competitor you'd like to "help.")

Assume for a moment that you ignored the warning signs (an unfriendly, uncommunicative prospect who wasn't clear on what he wanted and when he wanted it), and you decided to pursue it anyway. You can certainly argue that there's always a chance. But what about the odds, and does the time investment justify perhaps a 1-2% chance of getting lucky? Probably not. Be realistic. Remember, if it walks like a duck...

If they pass this early first hurdle, continue the qualifying process as detailed in the Common Sense Selling© system. Be aware, however, that the traffic lights can change at any time, and when they do, you will need to reevaluate whether continued involvement with the prospect is warranted.

Assuming all the lights are green at this point, you may be investing some serious time with the prospect, and the chances are good that, unless the lights start to turn red, you will be developing a proposal for your prospect.

One final thought on the warning signs – some prospects can be pretty convincing in the early stages of the relationship. Simply having all the lights appearing green does not necessarily mean that the road to winning the business will be easy. That's why it's important to continually evaluate the situation, look for roadblocks, and keep your antenna up for changes. Sometimes a healthy dose of skepticism is your best ally.

Red, or Green?

After you've completed your qualifying process, you must look at the traffic lights to determine whether or not to commit your time to developing a proposal for your prospective client. Here the prospect must pass your final test before you "reward" him with a proposal. (Yes, I said reward, because there is value in every proposal. Don't lose sight of that fact. Your proposal has value to your prospect in that it helps him evaluate the different options available to him.)

Your proposal also has value to you, since you invested time and other resources to develop it. Proposals aren't free (unless you treat them as having no value.)

So before you run off to spend time developing a proposal for anyone, take yourself through the following "pass or fail" mental exercise.

First, assume that it would cost you personally some significant monetary amount, such as $10,000, to develop a proposal and deliver it to the prospect. If it did, I suspect you'd want to be quite sure you had a very good chance for success; that you wouldn't invest $10,000 frivolously, right?

With that in mind, you would probably want to develop some rather strict guidelines that had to be met before making the $10,000 investment. Remember, the ten grand comes out of YOUR pocket!

There are six things you must know in order to let your prospect pass – in other words, before you reward your prospect with a proposal. Your ability to conduct a professional and complete qualification of your prospect during the meetings leading up to this point in the sales cycle will provide you with the answers. Here are the checkpoints.

1. You understand the <u>prospect's problem</u> thoroughly and are able to provide, at a minimum, a satisfactory solution.

If you don't understand the problem completely, how can you be sure you can suggest a solution that would be enthusiastically endorsed?

2. The prospect has to do something – it is NOT an option to keep things the same.

If keeping things the same is an option for the prospect, they might very well select that option. Problems tend to fall into the "fix it" or "forget it" categories. Unless there's a compelling reason to change, most find it easier just to do nothing. No pain, no change. Find the compelling reason why they'd want to go through the hassle of changing suppliers or implementing something new. If they can't present a compelling case for change, they probably won't change.

3. You have access to the decision maker and will make your presentation to him/her.

While this is covered in great detail in Chapter 11, Understanding the Decision Process, a good rule of thumb is never to make a presentation to someone who can't say "yes." It's that simple.

4. The prospect needs to implement a solution in a time frame that makes sense for you from a business standpoint.

Time kills deals. What's the point if your prospect doesn't want to do anything for 18 months? Too much can happen to in the interim to send the deal sideways.

5. You understand the prospect's selection criteria, and have a reasonable chance of meeting those criteria successfully.

What are the top three things they'll evaluate when selecting a business partner, and why are those things important? This will give you a good handle on just how good your chances are. If this is a price driven deal, for example, and you can't or won't compete on price alone, why try to compete at all? It's a very competitive world out there and your competitors are trying just as hard to win the business as you are. You've got to know their strengths and weaknesses, how they're likely to react in certain situations, how hard they'll fight for the opportunity that you're trying to win.

6. The prospect is considering only a small number of suppliers and is not putting the deal out to every company in the area.

Generally, "RFPs" are not the most optimum type of business to win, since price plays such a major role in the selection process and the opportunity to communicate openly with the prospect is often quite limited. Prospects whose attitude is "the more, the merrier" are more interested in price than a relationship. Finally, increasing the number of options for the prospect decreases your chances of winning.

Play the Odds

In many ways this is similar to what professional investors do. They have a strict set of rules for investing that tip the odds in their favor, and they know if they start ignoring those rules - playing hunches instead of playing the odds - they increase the risk of losing their investment.

Why take chances? If you can say "yes" to all six of these tough criteria, you have a very good chance of winning the business. If you must honestly answer "no" to any one of them, you may have seriously compromised your chances for winning, and need to reconsider whether investing your $10,000 is a smart business decision.

Let your prospect convince you that he's a good prospect.

3. Delivery

While proposals alone do not win the business for you, a "spot on" proposal can give you a big advantage. When somebody gives you exactly what you asked for it's kind of hard to say "no."

Somewhere during your qualification process you should have asked the prospect exactly what a perfect solution would look like. Let them describe their vision to you. Tailoring your offering so that it matches up as closely as possible to their vision of a solution is critical. Eliminating as many of the things they might object to increases the probability that they will say "yes."

If you can't give them exactly what they want, negotiate something that they agree would be an acceptable alternative before you make your proposal for the business. And if you can't negotiate an acceptable alternative, don't waste your time with a proposal that doesn't meet their needs. It's not any more complicated than this.

Leave Your Ego at Home

I attended an investment conference not too long ago and the presenter explained, in terms that I had not heard before, why most investors in the stock markets get "killed." They ignore the warning signs and their egos won't let them sell a stock that's going south on them. They rationalize that if they picked a stock, there must have been some very good reasons, so they'll stay with it just a bit longer in the hope that it will come back. Typically, that's a losing strategy.

Thinking you can beat the odds on a regular basis is foolish. In sales, hearing that your competitor won the business is always an ego crusher, especially after you've invested so much time on the opportunity.

Disqualifying them because they don't fit YOUR model is a much better strategy.

Summary

Can you ever be a 100% closer? Probably not. But will you get into the Hall of Fame by being a 20% closer? Certainly not. Strip away the roadblocks, do as many things right as possible, and, above all, be brutally honest about your chances.

Winning the business is playing the game smart; putting the odds in your favor. After all, it's not about quantity; it is about quality. As Kenny Rogers said in "The Gambler"…"You've got to know when to hold 'em – know when to fold 'em – know when to walk away and know when to run." Execute the Common Sense Selling© process faithfully and follow Kenny's advice and you just might make it into the "Closing Hall of Fame."

Oh. And don't forget to ask for the business. That's still good advice!

Chapter 13
Getting a Commitment

One of the major differences between traditional selling and Common Sense Selling® is that the real "close" comes before, not after, the presentation. It might seem like a small change, but it's a very important one. By asking the prospect what might happen if you made a presentation that completely and satisfactorily addressed all the issues, and the proposed solution fit the prospect's budget, you'll get an idea of just how close you are to the sale. You might even get a solid commitment at that point. You'll read more on this later.

In a simple, transactional sale the important points for closing are product availability and a reasonable (competitive) price. Trust between buyer and seller is normally irrelevant since there is no continuing relationship after the sale. Closing is typically an aggressive move calculated to get a positive response quickly. Pressure and manipulation are often associated with closing in a transactional sale.

In a complex, relationship based sale (typically higher dollar value), the buyer must trust the salesperson and company he represents. The buyer must have confidence that the salesperson understands his pain and the buyer must believe the pricing of the solution will provide satisfactory ROI.

"Closing" is a natural result when two people want to work together. It's a process (not an event) in a complex sale.

Each time the prospect decides to move forward in any way (agreeing that he has a problem and wants to find a solution, agreeing to spend money to fix the problem, agreeing to give you a decision when he sees your proposal), he's getting nearer and nearer to making a commitment because it makes sense and is the right thing to do.

The Closing Plan

The Closing Plan accomplishes two very important functions: it enables you to get a sense of what might happen if your presentation successfully addressed all the prospect's pain issues and it encourages the prospect to give you a clear decision at the end of your presentation.

The first part is to "test the waters" before you present your solutions. This will give you a clear indication of how ready your prospect is to accept your proposal if he perceives it as a good solution to his problems.

It might sound like this:

- "If you have the conviction that we can solve your problem and it makes sense financially, what will happen then?"

  or

- "If you felt that our solution was exactly what you need to eliminate these problems, and it fit your budget, what would you do at that point?"

If this sounds like a traditional "trial" close, it is, but with a twist. You're asking an open-ended question at the end to test the waters. You are not asking for a commitment from the prospect. The traditional trial close usually ends with, "Would you buy from me?" or "Would we have a deal?" It's a closing question and easily recognizable by the prospect as such. It's also a "set-up" question and adds pressure to the situation. It's unlikely that the prospect would say "no." In addition, you don't get any real feedback. Using an open-ended question to test the waters will often help you uncover additional information (like other decision makers, budget issues, etc.)

that you may have failed to discover during your earlier qualifying.

Our experience is that if the prospect does not respond positively with a buying commitment ("We'd have a deal"), he will give you valuable information that will help you understand where he is in the buying process and will expose areas in your qualification process where you failed to do a complete job. Examples of this might be:

- "I'd need to take it to my boss." (Oops, forgot to find out who really makes the decision.)
- "We'd have to get budgetary approval to move forward." (Darn, forgot to discuss whether or not they had a budget.)
- "We'll want to check out a couple of other vendors." (Wow, did I forget to ask about who else they were talking to?)

With this information you are now in a position to continue your qualifying effort and get answers to these and other issues that might be roadblocks to getting the business.

The second element of the Closing plan is to set up the conditions for a successful presentation.

Everybody needs to be on the same page for the presentation. No surprises. You've done a lot of hard work up to this point and you'd like a decision when you show the prospect your solutions. Think of it as *trading* a presentation for a decision. It's important to get a decision when you make your presentation because that's when the prospect is most enthusiastic. If you get a "think it over," you'll find that the enthusiasm starts to wane and the prospect will go from emotional to logical. Plus, you've done all the work and you deserve to get a decision.

Here's an example of how to express it: "Mr. Prospect, when we get together (next week, tomorrow, etc) for my presentation, here's what I would like to have happen.

First, let's make sure we have everybody who will have an impact on the final decision in the room. Then, I'll spend as much time as we need so that you can get a complete understanding of our solution and how it will solve your problem. I'll answer all your questions and you'll have everything you need to make a decision. When I'm done I expect you'll be feeling one of two ways. Either I've missed the point and this won't work for you, or this is the way we should go. So I hope that before I leave the meeting you will be able to tell me either 'yes' or 'no.' And by the way, I'm okay with a 'no' if you don't feel our proposal will work for you. All right?"

You will not always be able to get a decision when you make your presentation, but you will improve your chances if you ask. In any event, you must understand their decision process and timetable and agree on the appropriate follow up after you deliver your presentation. Don't settle for an ambivalent response like, "We'll get back to you." It's totally appropriate to ask for something more definitive.

In any sale where relationship is important, the salesperson must manage the "close" to a successful and natural conclusion. The objective is to eliminate pressure and obtain minor agreements throughout the process.

Key Points
1. Get a commitment before you make a presentation.
2. By asking the right questions, you can encourage the prospect to convince you he has a problem and wants to solve it.
3. You don't have to make a presentation (and probably shouldn't) if the prospect's commitment level is low.

Chapter 14
Winning Presentations

The presentation of your solutions should be very focused. This is not the time to do a feature/benefit "dump." Instead it is your opportunity to provide evidence to the prospect that your solutions will eliminate the challenges that he is dealing with. These challenges, of course, were uncovered when you were investigating for pain/motivation. The objective is to get a decision at the end of the presentation, plus address any issues that might cause the deal to fall through, such as buyer's remorse and/or competitive attempts to undermine your efforts.

Let's examine some of the key elements of delivering a winning presentation from a Common Sense Selling® perspective.

1. Never make a presentation to anyone who does not have the authority to make a decision. If the decision maker is not present, you cannot get a commitment. You can only get a "think it over" or worse, have someone with no authority tell you "no." Don't trust anyone to sell your solution for you. No one else can do it as well as you can. Nothing but problems will result when you don't present to the decision-maker.

2. Never make a presentation until you have completed the qualification process. You must understand the challenges (pains) they want you to help them resolve, you must have an idea about the monetary investment they would be comfortable with and you must understand their decision making process. Ideally, don't make your presentation unless the prospect has agreed to give you a decision. In the event that you can't get a decision at the end of your presentation, at least get a clear understanding of why they are unable to give you a decision and what your next step should be.

3. The goal of your presentation is to show the prospect exactly how you will eliminate his problems. You will provide whatever information is necessary to give the prospect the conviction that you are the right company to help them. However, this is not the time to do a gala feature & benefit extravaganza. Keep reading and you'll find out why.

A word of caution is necessary here for those overeager salespeople who just can't seem to stop talking. Never present anything to the prospect that does not relate directly to solving the challenges he has expressed. Additional, extraneous information may cause the presentation to get sidetracked, or worse give the prospect an opportunity to raise objections. A good rule of thumb is to fix the problems now, and save the "education" until later.

I recall a time when I was in corporate America selling inventory counting services to retailers. One of my salespeople and I were making a presentation to the decision maker of a very large grocery wholesaler in Oklahoma City. At one point during the presentation the buyer said to us, "I've heard enough. It's obvious to me that you'd be a good vendor for our retailers. Let's talk about getting the program set up." (In case you don't recognize it, that's called a "strong buying signal.") We'd made the sale, and it was time to get the contract signed. Unfortunately, my salesperson, a big talker if there ever was one, blurted out, "Wait. You haven't heard the best part."

Of course, that peaked the buyer's interest, and he asked, "Okay, what's the best part?" And my sales guy said, "It's our warranty. If we ever do a bad inventory, we'll come back and do another inventory for free."

"How often do you do bad inventories?" was the buyer's predictable retort. The focus of the meeting had changed in a heartbeat from getting the contract signed to defending the quality of our service, which, up to this time, had not been an issue. The momentum was lost for a few minutes and, although I was able to get it back on track, the sale could have been in jeopardy. One innocent little mistake can ruin everything.

So, when does the buyer learn about the warranty, you may be wondering? When, and if, there is ever a bad inventory, that's when. And just think about the positive points you'd make when you told him about that feature. There's a time and place for everything. Too much information can ruin a sale for you.

Presenting Your Solutions

Begin by reviewing the pain issues that the prospect wants to fix and ask the prospect which one you should discuss first. Whichever one he chooses is the most significant problem. Provide proof that you can fix it completely and gain the prospect's agreement that your solution is <u>completely</u> satisfactory. Don't move forward until you have agreement. Then, work on the remaining challenges in the same manner.

Testing for acceptance. Throughout your presentation you should continually "test" for acceptance by asking questions such as…

- "Are you with me so far?"
- "Does this make sense?"
- "Will this work for you?"
- "Do you have any reservations about this?"
- "How do you feel about what I've shown you?"

If you are doing a good job, you'll get positive responses. If you run into hesitation or concern on the prospect's part, deal with it before you move on.

The "Close." When the prospect gives you a strong buying signal, says something like "this looks great" or "this will work for us," your only "close" is: **"What should we do now?"** In other words, let the prospect close himself. No pressure. The best salespeople don't "close" the sale in the traditional sense, they bring it to a natural conclusion.

Protecting The Sale

Most salespeople breathe a sigh of relief once the prospect has agreed to buy. However, don't be misled into a false sense of security. All of your hard work can still be undone by buyer's remorse, competition or some other roadblock. Deal with them before you leave to make sure you don't lose the sale tomorrow. Here are some ideas.

Buyer's Remorse. Second-guessing our decision - we've all had buyer's remorse at some point or another. It generally comes from being pressured into buying something against our better judgment. Of course, pressure is not a part of Common Sense Selling®, so buyer's remorse should not be an issue. Nevertheless, you should check for buyer's remorse before you leave. You might say, "Before I leave I'd like to make sure you are totally comfortable with what we've agreed to do. If you are not, if you have any hesitation whatsoever, let's talk about it." Nine times out of ten your new customer will reaffirm his decision to do business with you. But if he does have some unresolved issues, you are there to deal with them.

Competitive Retaliation. The incumbent that you have displaced or other companies that were competing with you for the business may fire off one last shot in an attempt to keep or win the business. Normally the tactic of choice is to reduce their price, but other incentives could be offered as well. Unfortunately, there are times when this tactic is successful and you'll get a call from your new "customer" saying, "I just got a call from XYZ company and they've lowered their prices. It's a significant savings and I'll have to go with them unless you can match their price." Now that's a call we all love to get, isn't it?

Here's how to deal with it. "Head 'em off at the pass," so to speak. In a highly competitive situation, after your prospect has committed his business to you, you should say to your customer, "Thanks for giving us the business. I appreciate it. But, you know, I have one concern that I'd like to share with you if I might." Your customer will ask you what it is, of course. And you'll reply, "This has been a very competitive situation, as you know, and I'm wondering just what your current vendor will do when they find out that you're giving your business to us. What do you think they'll do?"

A typical reply might be, "Well, they'll probably come back in and offer us a better deal or some other incentive to stay with them." Your response, simply, is, "If they do that, what will you do?"

This tough question takes some guts because you're testing for bad news. If they say that they'd have to consider it, then you know that the sale is not made. But at least you're there, face to face, to deal with the situation. That sure beats getting the voice mail (date and time stamped well before or after office hours so they don't have to talk you) saying, "Sorry, our current vendor offered us a better deal and we're going to stay with them." All your hard work - down the drain.

But, in reality, it's usually not bad news when you ask that tough question. If you've done a great job qualifying, found lots of pain and positioned yourself as a true resource to them and not just a product pusher, you'll feel great when they tell you that they have no intention of changing their mind because you are the best choice for them. Once they've made that commitment to you it's more difficult for them to go back on their word.

Roadblocks. Several years ago we were training a large technology company. Their prospects who had decision-making authority were typically C level executives, usually the CTO (Chief Technical Officer) or CIO (Chief Information Officer) and the average sale was in the mid-six figures. A major problem that this tech company expressed to us was that after the executive made the decision to buy from them, he would create a PO and it would go to the Purchasing Department. There it would often get stalled. Purchasing, wanting to be diligent, sometimes would send the PO out to bid or bring in the vendor to negotiate price or terms. This would, at best, stall the sale and, at worst, cause the entire sales process to start anew.

We suggested that in these situations they ask the prospect what roadblocks they might incur in getting the project implemented. They may mention one or two, and if they don't, we might even bring one up, such as the potential problem with purchasing. If the prospect mentions that something could be a roadblock, then we ask the prospect how he will deal with the roadblock. This approach puts ownership of the problem where it belongs, on the prospect.

Key Points
1. Trade a presentation for a decision.
2. If it's not important to them, don't tell them about it.
3. Protect the sale from buyer's remorse and competitive retaliation.

Chapter 15
Becoming a Master Communicator

Communication skills are the key to being successful in sales. They serve two important purposes. First, they help you understand the prospect's challenges (pain). Second, by focusing the conversation on the prospect, you are able to build a high level of trust and minimize the perception of self-interest.

Communication is a two-way street. That is, it involves both speaking and listening. Salespeople must have the skills to keep the focus on the prospect, to keep the prospect talking, to be a good listener and build a trusting relationship with the prospect. After all, your job is to get information, not give it. How else can you diagnose the prospect's challenges effectively? If the diagnosis is flawed, how much confidence will your prospect have in the solution?

When you are talking you are saying something that <u>you</u> already know. When you listen you discover something that someone else knows. Many attempts to communicate are nullified by saying too much.

If you want to interact with someone communication is essential. If you want to influence or advise someone understanding his or her point of view is critical. A good rule of thumb is to keep your prospect speaking twice as much as you do. After all, you have two ears and one mouth and you should use them in that ratio in professional selling. Unfortunately, most salespeople are like alligators – all mouth and no ears.

Amateur to Professional – The Questioning Progression

As someone who sells gains experience, their questioning skills seem to develop in a rather predictable manner.

The following is *not* to suggest that this is the *correct* way to build your skills. It is, however, fairly representative of how salespeople mature in their questioning skills. Which phase best describes your questioning skills?

Phase 1. Talk, talk, talk. The beginner salesperson, like the aforementioned alligator, is all mouth and no ears. Eager to show his product knowledge, he monopolizes the conversation. His principle tactic is to demonstrate his enthusiastic belief in his product or service. He makes a lot of presentations and occasionally closes one or two. Asking questions is a skill the rookie has not yet mastered.

AL E. GATOR, ALL MOUTH AND NO EARS

Phase 2. Closed end questions. Recognizing that he needs to ask questions, he grudgingly relents but limits his efforts to a few closed end questions, those that solicit only a yes or no answer. This fishing expedition represents some progress, certainly, but the information he gets is severely limited. Examples are:

- "Are you happy with your current supplier?"
- "Are you in the market for (my product or service)?"
- "Are you familiar with my company?"

It's important to note that the answers often do not elicit the response we're looking for. ("Yes, I am happy with my current supplier. If I wasn't I'd have done something about it." *Oops, what do I do now?)*

Phase 3.   Manipulative questions.   Having learned quickly that these questions need some serious work, the amateur decides to get some help. He buys a book on basic selling skills or solicits help from an "experienced" colleague.   The book often is one that has been in print forever and thus qualifies for "best seller" status; it typically suggests tactics that are outdated.   The "experienced" colleague is often another salesperson who has been making the same mistakes for many years but nevertheless "qualifies" as an expert. The expert is eager to show the rookie some "great sales moves" that, in reality, are not so great.   Armed with this advice from the "experts," the rookie makes the transition from innocent to shark. Manipulative questions are the new tool of choice. Manipulative questions attempt to "set-up" the prospect by soliciting only the answers that are favorable to the salesperson's cause. Examples are:

- "You'd be interested in saving time and money, wouldn't you?" (very generic)
- "You wouldn't want your family to suffer in the event of your untimely death, would you?" (life insurance)
- "You wouldn't want to miss out on a good investment opportunity, would you?" (investments)

113

The problem with these questions is that they are over-used and put a great deal of pressure on the prospect. Let's face it, who wouldn't be interested in saving time and money or protecting their family? How can someone say "no" to that? That's the point, it corners the prospect and a cornered prospect feels pressure and will look for any excuse to get rid of the salesperson that created the pressure. These questions may find some success in a low value, transactional sale, but they will get you thrown out of many prospects' offices too.

Phase 4. Open-ended questions. The first major breakthrough is to master the use of open ended-questions – questions that must be answered with more than a simple "yes" or "no." The six principal open-ended interrogatives are who, when, where, what, why and how. These are, as the British writer, Rudyard Kipling, said, your "six faithful serving men."

- *"Who* will be part of the decision making process on this initiative?"
- *"When* do you need to get a solution implemented?"
- *"Where* are the system users located?"
- *"What* are the major challenges you're facing in growing your sales?"
- *"Why* did you decide to invest in this technology?"
- *"How* will you evaluate the options available to you?"

From the above examples, you can begin to see how, by using open-ended questions, you will receive far better information than from closed-ended questions. In addition, the focus will shift from the salesperson, to the prospect, which is where it needs to be in a relationship sale.

The "Uncooperative" Prospect

So far this all sounds very simple - just ask open-ended questions. However, prospects have their own agenda and it's designed, as we have previously said, to get as much information as possible from the salesperson. Questions are their tool of choice as well. The momentum can change quickly unless the salesperson possesses the skills to keep the prospect talking.

The person asking the questions is the one who controls the conversation. The salesperson must be able to maintain control when the prospect says, "Tell me about your company" or "How would you solve a problem like this?" without falling into the trap of making a premature presentation.

This leads us into the next two phases of the questioning progression which, when mastered, start to move us into the realm of professional selling.

Phase 5. Rewarding and refocusing. Reversing the flow of information when the prospect decides to start picking the salesperson's brain is a tactic that takes skill and practice. Making the transition is key. It involves an acknowledgment followed by a question. Here's an example.

> Prospect: "How long does the installation take?"
> Salesperson: "I'm glad you asked. Are there some timing issues I need to be aware of?"

Simply providing an answer is an inviting option, especially when the answer is easy and may put you in a favorable light. However, the trap you may fall into is that it can open up the floodgates and put a premature end to qualifying the prospect. Using this tactic, the salesperson has "rewarded" the prospect with "I'm glad you asked" and "refocused" the conversation to the possible time restraints the prospect is facing. This keeps the salesperson in control by continuing to ask questions and minimizes the potential for unpaid consulting.

This tactic is not intended to be evasive. Sometimes a short answer is appropriate, but the key is to always follow up with a question. Example:

> Prospect: "What is your policy on warranty returns?"
> Salesperson: "I'm glad you asked me that. We have a 30-day return policy. What's been your experience with warranties with your current vendor?"

You will maintain control of the sales conversation and, ultimately, your destiny by learning how to reward and refocus. Remember, the best investigators close the most business.

Phase 6. Easy Exits (Takeaways). In martial arts the defender uses the attacker's momentum against him. This involves doing the unexpected; beating the adversary at his own game. In selling, it's quite counterintuitive, but incredibly effective.

Instead of following the traditional selling tactic of trying to *push* the prospect into buying, the salesperson does the opposite, giving the prospect an "easy exit." It's very disarming and completely removes any pressure to buy. Freed of pressure, prospects often open up and share more information than they ordinarily would.

An additional benefit is that the salesperson can *never* stumble when using this liberating technique, as you'll see.

> Prospect: "This is not that big a problem for us."
> Salesperson: "Well then, maybe we should close the file if you can live with the situation the way it is."

116

Prospect: "No, we've got to do something about it."

It's easy to see how the traditional salesperson might try to convince the prospect to reconsider his position. He'd try to sell harder and overcome the prospect's reluctance. He'd probably say something like, "It may not be that big a problem now, but if you don't do something, you might be sorry later." If you were the prospect, would you be likely to agree with the salesperson or would you start to feel some pressure and try to defend your position? Do you see why trying to overcome the objection and sell harder seldom works?

By the way, if you're not going to win the sale, then lose it early. If the prospect had agreed that the problem was not worth spending time on, as the salesperson suggested, then wouldn't it be smart to move on?

We've progressed nearly full circle in the six phases of questioning. We've gone from the amateur who does all the talking to the professional who can get the prospect to convince him he has a problem and wants to solve it.

The Other Half of the Equation

Next to survival, one of the greatest needs we have as human beings is the need to be understood. People need to trust you in a selling situation. They need to feel comfortable opening up to you and sharing their concerns, fears and hopes. You need to be a trusted advisor to succeed in sales.

Salespeople seem to spend most of their time in *transmit* mode. They should spend most of their time in *receive* mode. We must be good listeners to succeed at sales.

Basically we communicate in four ways. We speak, we write, we read and we listen. The first three we learned in school, but we're not taught much about becoming better listeners.

Many people are poor listeners, even though it is one of the most prized inter-personal skills. We typically listen at one of five levels:

1. Ignoring
2. Pretending we're listening ("Yeah, uh huh...")
3. Selective listening (only hearing parts of what's being said)
4. Attentive listening (paying attention; focusing on the words being said and how best to reply)
5. Empathetic listening (listening with the intent to understand; getting inside their frame of reference)

Poor listening habits can lead to numerous misunderstandings and conflicts. Research indicates that, on average, we retain about 50% of the main content of a ten-minute speech immediately after listening to it. A conservative estimate is that most people retain no more than 25% of what they hear after two days.

Poor Listening Habits

All of us have some poor listening habits that we may be able to get away with when talking to family or friends. In a business environment, however, one must leave these bad habits behind. Here are just a few common bad habits.

- Monopolizing the conversation
- Interrupting
- Putting words in someone's mouth
- Finishing sentences for people if they pause too long
- Asking a question about something that's already been covered, showing you weren't listening
- Exhibiting a poker face that keeps people wondering if you are paying attention
- Toying with a pencil or some other item while people are talking
- Arguing

Every one of these sends a clear message to your conversation partner that they are not important to you and, as such, contributes to lowering levels of trust and rapport.

Active Listening

Active listening is a skill that requires continual practice. Being an active listener demonstrates to the other person that you are interested in what they are saying and that you understand both the content and the feeling of their message. With this feedback your conversation partner is more willing to give you the information you are seeking. The dialogue becomes collaborative, not adversarial.

There are seven primary types of active listening, listed from least to most effective. Assume for the examples below the prospect said the following:

"We won't hit our numbers this year."

Response	Basic Premise	Examples
Non-verbal	Conveys interest using only body language	Nodding head, leaning forward
Neutral	Non-committal words that encourage person to keep talking	"Uh-huh" "I see"
Mimicking	Parroting back the content exactly as heard	"You won't hit your numbers this year."
Restating	Changing the words slightly	"So you won't hit your plan?"
Reflecting	Describing how the person seems to feel	"Sounds like you're upset."
Encouraging	Asking well placed open-ended questions to get more information	"Tell me more." "What else is there?"
Summarizing	Summarizing the ideas and the feelings	"You seem quite frustrated by your company's performance this year."

It's far better to be interested, than to be interesting. There are two types of people – you know them well. Those who come into a room and say, "Well, here I am," and those who come in and say, "Ah, there you are." Which one are you?

Key Points
1. You can't put your foot in your mouth if it's closed.

2. What your prospect has to say is more important than what you have to say.
3. You won't learn anything if you do all the talking.
4. The person who is asking the questions is in control of the conversation and the direction of the meeting.

Chapter 16
The Tactics Toolbox

A carpenter has many implements in his toolbox; hammer, screwdriver, chisel, wrench, saw, pliers, etc. For each job he knows exactly which tools to use to complete the job quickly and effectively. Similarly, a medical professional knows various treatment options to prescribe, depending on the diagnosis and severity of the illness. It's the same in selling...the more tools or tactics you've mastered, the more successful you'll be - once you've assessed the situation.

There are a number of great tactics that can be used to handle a wide variety of stalls, objections and roadblocks. We've listed a few of them here. Think of them as your selling tool kit. The secret to being a true professional is to understand how the tactics work and to know when to use them.

Let's take a look at the options you have available with your Common Sense Selling® tactics tool kit.

Reward and Refocus

Your job, as a sales professional, is to get as much information as possible when you are qualifying an opportunity. Yet your prospective client feels *his* job is to do the same when he is exploring his alternatives while not exposing any weakness that might put him at a disadvantage. The salesperson *must* have superior questioning skills.

On a typical appointment, your prospect has a number of questions that he has prepared to ask you in order to determine if you are a company that he might want to do business with. We've discussed in previous chapters how adept prospects are at turning salespeople into "unpaid consultants." In order for you to achieve your objective of being a great investigator and obtaining lots of information, we suggest a tactic called rewarding and refocusing. It enables you to answer the prospect's question or respond to a statement with a question of your own, subtly reversing the flow of information from the prospect and back to you.

A reward functions as a transition from the prospect's question to yours, such as, "That's a good question" or "I'm glad you asked me that." The reward is then followed by a question that relates to the prospect's question. The purpose is to keep the prospect talking until you can obtain enough information to deal with the issue effectively. It might sound like this:

> Prospect: "How would you solve a problem like this?"
> You: "That's a good question. What have you tried so far?"
> Prospect: "Well, we've ..."

A word of clarification is necessary here. This tactic is not designed to be deceptive or manipulative. In fact, sometimes a *short answer* followed by a question is quite appropriate. "We've found that.....works quite well. What have you tried?"

The Easy Exit or Takeaway

This tactic is very misunderstood by many, since it seems to give the prospect an easy exit by pushing him toward a "no." It is behaving in a manner that is contradictory to what a prospect would expect a salesperson to do, and as such, is very disarming. Using reverse psychology, it subconsciously encourages the prospect to be truthful. It puts the prospect in a position to disagree with something "negative" said by the salesperson, thereby turning the area in question to a positive. Here's an example:

Prospect: "That's really more than we wanted to invest."

Salesperson: "I get the feeling you don't feel we'll be able to work together. Maybe I should just close the file."

Prospect: "No, we really like your program. It's just that our budget is a little tight right now. Can you help us with some payment terms?"

Did you notice how the prospect "refused" to let the salesperson close the file? The prospect went from a price objection to saying he liked the program; it happened because the salesperson did the unexpected and removed the pressure. The prospect provided the momentum to move the sale forward. The salesperson simply got out of the way.

DON'T SET THE HOOK TOO SOON.

It doesn't happen that way all the time, but you'd be amazed at how often "going negative" gets the prospect to "go positive."

Colombo

This tactic is especially useful when you need to get more information. It involves acting somewhat confused (on purpose) in order to encourage your prospect to open up and clarify a particular issue. Lt. Colombo (Peter Falk) used this approach to perfection. It is totally disarming and puts the prospect in a position to help you, the "confused" salesperson, get things straight. It sounds like this:

> Prospect: "We've decided to wait a month or two to make our decision."
> Salesperson: "I'm a little confused. You said this problem was costing you $10,000 a month and was top priority fix. Can you help me understand why you want to delay now? I must be missing something."
> Prospect: "Well, here's the real problem..."

Third Party Stories

It's very helpful to talk about a similar experience that you've had with another client in order to gain credibility. If you think back, it's fairly easy to come up with something that correlates. Here's an example:

> Prospect: "I'm not sure your training will work for our people who live over an hour from your training center."
> Salesperson: "I understand your concern. Interestingly, we had a very similar situation with a client about three months ago, and we did a combination of telephone classes and in-house

125

training. It's exceeded their expectations. Others have carpooled. Would either one work for you?"
Prospect: "It's possible. Let's explore it further."

If You Sense It, Say It (Nicely)

Have you ever said to yourself during a sales call, "I get the feeling that...."? Sometimes your intuition tells you that something is wrong and needs to be discussed, but you don't know how or are not comfortable bringing it up. The following are fairly common issues that fit this category.
- Their budget may be inadequate to address the problem.
- There may be others who will influence or make the decision.
- The problem they're talking about really is not all that serious or may not be the <u>real</u> problem.
- They have a long-standing relationship with an existing vendor and it would be difficult for them to make a change.

It's important to deal with the issue early on before it becomes a bigger problem or even a deal breaker. You might say something like this...

Salesperson: "Sue, I'm not sure why, but I get the feeling that it would be very difficult for you to make a change, given the long standing relationship you've had with your current supplier."
Prospect: "Well, we have had a good relationship with them, that's true. But recently they've had some quality problems and we've got to look at alternatives."
Salesperson: "Really. Are you sure that wouldn't be a problem?"
Prospect: "No. It's pretty serious."

Let's Pretend (Future Decision)

If you have trouble moving people forward and getting them to make a decision, then this tactic is for you. It involves taking the prospect into the future, presenting a hypothetical solution and asking them to make a decision. It's a great test for commitment and a good "smoke detector." It sounds like this:

> Salesperson: "Let's pretend that it was two weeks from now and I had just finished showing you how we were going to address the problems you're facing. During the presentation you came to the conclusion that our solution was just what you needed and it fit your budget. What would happen then?"
> Prospect: "I'd buy it."

You may be thinking that it can't be that simple to get a buying commitment. While they might not respond as positively as this, at the very least you will have a good sense of how close you are to being successful.

The Scale

How often do you hear a trial close or test for acceptance by saying, "Well, what do you think about the proposal?" Often is the response something ambivalent like, "Not too bad" or "It's OK."? And you say to yourself, "What does that mean?." Then you try to close because it seems like the only thing left to do, and you blow it.

The problem is that you lack good information and need to clarify what your prospect really means. Clearly a new tactic is in order. If you'd like a little clarity, try the scale. This tactic involves asking the prospect to provide you with a numerical value to describe how he feels about your proposal. You can do this before you are finished with your presentation or anytime you want to get a reading on your prospect. It might go like this:

> Salesperson: "It seems like we're making some progress, but I'm not exactly sure if I'm completely meeting your expectations. Can I ask you a question?
> Prospect: "Sure."
> Salesperson: "On a scale of one to ten, with ten being you're ready to hire us, where are you?"
> Prospect: "About a seven."
> Salesperson: "Seven. Sounds like we're making progress, but still have some work to do. What do you need to see to be more comfortable with our proposal?"
> Prospect: "Well, I need to get more comfortable about how you would handle the warranties."
> Salesperson: "And that would do it, that's all?"
> Prospect: "Yes."

Tactics are the tools you need to deal effectively with the unexpected situations your prospects throw at you. Selling is a business where having a slight edge is important, and these tactics can give you the slight edge that keeps you in the game when you might otherwise be at a loss for what to do. Tactics are not intended to be manipulative; instead, see them as a way to further communication between you and your prospects and customers.

Key Points
1. The more tactics you have mastered, the easier your job will be.
2. Questions are your most effective tools.
3. Listen to your prospect's answers; they'll provide you with a roadmap to your destination.

Chapter 17
Damage Control -
Dealing With Stalls & Objections

Most sales training programs have focused heavily on teaching salespeople how to overcome objections. Tactics like "reducing to the ridiculous," "isolate and validate," "feel/felt/found," the "Ben Franklin close" and "changing the base" were introduced to give salespeople the means to deal with the objections they were getting. And, after the tactic was employed it was followed by a trial close.

The problem with using these approaches is that the prospect has heard them all before and sees them as manipulative efforts to force him to change his mind. They were created for a simple, transactional type of sale, and when used in a more complex sale, they usually are not very effective and may create a wary prospect.

Consider this. When a prospect objects to something (for example, he doesn't need some of the features that your product has) the typical salesperson starts selling harder. This forces the prospect to defend his position. When someone starts to defend their position, they are further and further away from buying. Often the salesperson's "best" efforts create a more negative prospect.

Causes of Objections

There are several fundamental causes of stalls and objections. The principal cause is that the prospect is not willing or able to make a decision at this point in their buying process. If their buying cycle is not in synch with the salesperson's "selling" cycle (in other words, the salesperson needs to make the sale more than the buyer needs to make the purchase), the prospect may find something to object to so that the sales process can be delayed.

A second cause is that the prospect doesn't trust the salesperson. He may see the salesperson as just another commission crazed pitchman. But even so he doesn't want to hurt the salesperson's feelings, so he devises something to object to in order not to have to buy. People buy from people they like and trust, and if the trust factor is low, buyers often resort to concocting some sort of roadblock in an attempt to end the process.

Finally, often the salesperson has provided the prospect with too much information too soon – premature presentation. It all gets back to "salesperson's disease," their propensity to "show up and throw up." Simply put, if we don't offer information, the prospect can't object to it. To be more specific, if we don't divulge our price, can the prospect say it's too expensive? If we don't tell him all the features of our product or service, can he compare us unfavorably to our competition? Simply keeping your mouth shut can help you avoid half the objections that you get.

Before we apply the tactics you learned in the previous chapters, there are two additional tactics that you should master in order to be able to maintain control and handle any objection that you might get with total confidence.

Landmines

The military clears a minefield before they move forward. They know (or suspect) the landmines exist and realize that not to clear them would spell disaster. Selling is no different. Often we suspect that a landmine exists, that there is an objection or roadblock that is likely to surface at some point in the sales process, but we typically ignore it in the hopes that it will disappear. Most of the time it doesn't.

Don't ignore landmines; deal with them as soon as possible. For example, one of our commercial banking clients was frustrated with deals collapsing at the last minute when the prospect got cold feet because of all the hassle involved in changing banks. For a large company, it is a big deal and creates lots of extra work and confusion. Sometimes it's easier to live with the problems – as long as they aren't major.

We taught the bankers we work with to deal with this potential roadblock up front. Whenever they began a dialogue with a new prospect, they said, "Changing banks can be a big hassle. I know that you've said that you're not totally happy with your current bank, but my biggest concern is that we'll both spend a lot of time exploring the options with each other and, even if we can provide a better program than they can offer you, you'll tell me at the end of the process that it's just too big a hassle to change banks. What's the likelihood of that happening?"

You might be concerned that this approach would permit the prospect to say that it would, indeed, be a big hassle to change and lead to a premature conclusion of the sales opportunity. You'd be wrong. This question is absolutely key to assessing just how committed the prospect is to making a change. If that commitment is not there, you'd be better off finding out sooner than later.

This tactic works well when you want to deal with any landmine before it explodes. Other times when it can be effective are:

- When you think you might be denied access to the decision maker
- When you are worried that the final decision will be based solely on price and low price is not your strong suit
- When you suspect that you are just being used to provide a proposal so that the prospect can use it to negotiate a better deal with your competitor

A word of caution. This is not intended to be an "in your face" tactic. It must be delivered with great skill and humility or you will risk alienating some prospects.

Divide and Conquer

A mistake that many salespeople make is attempting to handle the objection as soon as it comes up. Then they find themselves dealing with another objection and another after that. When you hear an objection, determine if it is the only one or if there are others. Then you'll know where you stand.

Simply say to the prospect, "Yes, we need to talk about that. But, before we do, is there anything else that you're concerned about or is this it?"

If the prospect says there are others, find out what they are and which is most critical. If this is the only one, it's appropriate to say, "Assuming we can deal successfully with that issue, what would you do at that point?"

Now, let's get some answers and options to the twelve most common stalls and objections that salespeople have to deal with. Notice how the traditional salesperson responds and how different and effective our suggestions are.

The Most Common Stalls & Objections
- "Just send me some information."
- "I need to think it over."
- "Your price is too high."
- "I haven't had time to look at it."
- "It just isn't a priority right now."
- "We've had a bad experience with your company."
- "We're happy with our current supplier."
- "I need to talk to my boss to get approval."
- "We've never heard of your company."
- "I don't like the way (mentions something specific)"

132

- "I need to get some other quotes."

In the following pages you'll see just how different these tactics are from the traditional approaches. You'll see the objection, see how most salespeople might respond to it, and then see a variety of possible responses from the tactics that you've just learned. Make up your mind which one(s) might work best for you.

You may not agree with all the options we've listed and that's okay. Just keep your mind open to the possibilities, not the limitations. Here they are:

"Just send me some information."

Traditional Response: "Okay. I'll call you next week to follow up."

Reward & Refocus: "I'd be glad to do that. Can you tell me specifically what you would like to have information about? (Prospect responds.) That's interesting, why is that important?"

The Takeaway: "Sometimes when people ask me to send information they're really telling me they're not very interested, but just don't know how to tell me that. Is that the case here?"

Colombo: "I'm a little confused. Why would you want me to send information?"

Let's Pretend: "Let's pretend I sent you some information and you liked what you saw. What would happen then?"

"I need to think it over."

Traditional Response #1: "Exactly what do you need to think over?"

Traditional Response #2: "The price is going up next week. Don't you think you should act now?"

Traditional Response #3: 'Bill, this is the last one we have in stock. You wouldn't want to miss out would you?"

Reward & Refocus: "I understand. Was there something that I failed to cover adequately that we need to discuss further?"

Sense It & Say It: "I get the feeling that you really don't have any interest in my product? Is that a fair statement?"

The Scale: "Bob, you sound like you have a lot of indecision about this. Let me ask you this question...on a scale of one to ten, with ten being you're ready to do business with us, where are you?"

The Takeaway: "Bob, often when people tell me they need to think it over I find that they really are trying to tell me 'no,' but they just don't want to hurt my feelings. Is that the case here?"

"Your price is too high."

Traditional Response #1: "Yes, but when you consider the savings it's really a good investment."

Traditional Response #2: "Well, if we can get the price a little lower, would we have a deal?"

Traditional Response #3: "Actually when you look at the cost per day it's less than one dollar."

134

Reward & Refocus: "Sounds like that's a real issue for you. Can you help me understand how far out of the ballpark we are?

Reward & Refocus: "Meagan, let's assume for a moment that price wasn't an objection for you. What other issues would we have to resolve before we could look seriously at working together?"

Reward & Refocus: "I appreciate your candor. Is price the only issue?"

The Takeaway: "Bob, I get the feeling that you may have completely eliminated us because of the price issue. Is that true?"

Colombo: "Too high? Now I'm really confused. I thought price was the least important criteria in your purchase. What am I missing? Can you help me out?"

Let's Pretend: "Rick, suppose our prices weren't too high, what other concerns do you have?"

"I haven't had time to look at it."

Traditional Response: "I'll call you back in a couple of days then and we can discuss it. OK?"

Sense It & Say It and Takeaway: "Sue, I get the feeling that it's not very high on your list of priorities. Should we just close the file?"

Reward & Refocus: "It sounds like you've been busy. When will you have a chance to look at it?"

"It just isn't a priority right now."

135

Traditional Response: "But we can really help you _____, and I can probably find a way to shave a little off the price if you'll buy it now."

Reward & Refocus: "I guess I'm not surprised to hear that, Jim. Can you help me understand what would have to happen to make it a higher priority?"

Colombo: "Bill, I'm a little confused by your statement. I thought you told me last week that it was important to address these issues. What happened? Has something changed or did I simply misunderstand?"

The Takeaway: "I understand. Should we close the file then?"

"We've had a bad experience with your company."

Traditional Response: "Things have changed a lot at the company recently. We are doing a lot better in the service area these days."

Reward & Refocus: "I see. Can you tell me what happened?"

The Takeaway: "I'm aware of that incident. Based on that, I'd be surprised if you'd even give us another chance."

Sense It & Say It: "Since you brought that up, I get the feeling that we'd have little chance to do business together again. Am I right?"

"We're happy with our current supplier."

Traditional Response: "I understand how you feel. Lots of people have felt that way, but most have found that when they start using our products they are able to improve/save/eliminate _____. I'm sure you'll feel the same way if you work with us too."

Reward & Refocus: "Not unusual. They're a good company. Could they be doing anything better?"

The Takeaway and Sense It & Say It: "Not unusual, they're a good company. Frankly, I get the feeling that there's no way you'd ever consider making a change. What do you think?"

Colombo: "I'm a little confused. Does that mean that you're not open to considering another alternative?"

"I need to talk to my boss to get approval."

Traditional Response: "OK. When should I call you to see what she says?"

Reward & Refocus: "Jan, I appreciate your telling me that, but I'm curious. What will you recommend to your boss when you speak to her?"

The Takeaway: "Tom, don't take this the wrong way, but the last time someone told me that they were really trying to say that they just weren't interested. Is that where you are?"

Colombo: "Gosh, I'm kind of confused. I thought you had the final authority to approve this purchase. Did I miss something?"

Let's Pretend: "Jan, let's assume your boss says we should go ahead. What happens then?"

The Scale: "I understand. But let me ask you, on a scale of one to ten, with ten being you'd buy it if it were your decision, how do you feel about our proposal?"

"We've never heard of your company."

Traditional Response: "We're a leading (up and coming) provider of _____, and we've helped many companies just like yours improve/save/eliminate ....."

Reward & Refocus: "I see. I'm curious, what do you look for in a supplier?"

The Takeaway: "I get the feeling that you'd probably try to avoid doing business with an unknown. Have you had a bad experience in the past?"

Third Party Story: "It's true we're a relative newcomer. In fact, we met with a company just last week that had the same concern, but they discovered that our technology was just what they needed. If you came to feel that way, would the fact that we're a young company still be a barrier to us working together?"

"I don't like the way you (mentions something specific)"

Traditional Response: "Yes, but you'll find that our approach gets excellent results."

Reward & Refocus: "That sounds important. Can you tell me a little more about your concerns?"

The Takeaway: "Really. Should I assume from that comment that you've decided not to use us?"

"I need to get some other quotes."

Traditional Response #1: "Okay, but I think you'll find that our prices are quite competitive, especially when you consider the overall value."

Traditional Response #2: "Well, I could come down a little. Would that help?"

Sense It & Say It (plus Reward & Refocus)
"Bill, I get the feeling that our proposal really missed the mark. Is it a price issue or something else?"

The Takeaway (after the prospect responds to the above tactic): "Should we close the file or should we try to see if we can find a solution that works for both of us? Your choice."

If you learn these new tactics and how to apply them to the stalls and objections that you receive regularly you'll find yourself more confident, more in control and closing more business.

Key Points
1. The less information you volunteer, the fewer objections you'll receive.
2. Identify the landmines and clear the minefield as soon as you can.
3. Divide and conquer. Make sure you understand all the objections before proceeding to solve them.

Chapter 18
Negotiating Tips

In a business-to-business environment negotiating can be everything from a simple, one issue give and take to a very complex process requiring multiple meetings. Since most salespeople seldom "sit down across the negotiating table," our intent here is to provide you with some basic negotiating tactics that will help you level the playing field.

Yes, level the playing field. Most salespeople are woefully unprepared to negotiate, since they are too emotionally involved in the outcome. They simply want the business too badly to be objective.

Common Negotiating Mistakes

Virtually all the experts would agree that that the following mistakes are commonplace when salespeople start to negotiate. Awareness of these challenges may improve your ability to negotiate considerably.

- **Getting emotionally involved.** This one tops the list because, above all, your attitude toward something determines your success. If you appear needy, conveying the message to your prospect that you'll do almost anything to get the business, your prospect will sense this weakness and exploit it. Avoid statements like, "We'd really like to get this done," "I need this to make my quota this month," "What do we need to do to get you to buy from us?," etc. All indicate you are willing to do most anything to get the prospect to buy, and the smart prospect will try to see how far you actually will go. Remember, credibility is key in negotiations!
- **Making unilateral concessions.** A unilateral concession is agreeing to a prospect's request too quickly, and without asking for something of equal

or greater value in return. For example, your prospect asks you to lower your price by 5%. Your response is, "Sure, we can do that." Put yourself in your prospect's shoes and reflect on what message your response sent. First, he's undoubtedly thinking that since you agreed so easily, he should have asked for more. Second, he knows that since you dropped your prices so easily, you've probably overpriced the product or service. This creates doubt about the overall quality of what you're selling. Finally, you've demonstrated your inexperience as a negotiator, opening yourself for more abuse as the negotiation goes on.

- **Not understanding the prospect's pain and his alternatives.** This is your "ace in the hole" and without it you are defenseless. As we've previously mentioned in this book, most salespeople qualify poorly, betting on their powers of persuasion, features and benefits and charming personalities to get the job done. That doesn't work. It's very difficult, if not impossible, to stand your ground if you don't know what the prospect's downside is if the problem is not fixed. Therefore, you must uncover how severe their pain is, how it impacts both the company and the individual you're negotiating with, and what happens if the problem doesn't get resolved through negotiations.

- **Talking too much.** When you are monopolizing the conversation it's impossible to "read" your adversary or learn what their specific needs are. You're giving information, not receiving it. Falling into this trap is a sure way to lose.

- **Not understanding your objectives and value items.** Failure to have worked out, in advance, your list of primary (best case) and secondary (fall back) objectives will create confusion and indecision for

141

you. If you don't, you'll just end up winging it.
This is a surefire road to disaster.

The Buyer's Tactics

If you've ever thumbed through an airline magazine
you've seen the ads for negotiating workshops. They
appeal primarily to buyers and, consequently, buyers often
are far more prepared than most salespeople. Let's explore
some of *their* tactics.

- **Playing one supplier off against the other.** This
  is the oldest trick in the book. But it's an effective
  one since salespeople tend to take the prospect at
  his word, despite the fact that occasionally
  prospects mislead salespeople. Unfortunately
  there's nothing in the rulebook that says the
  prospect has to be able to prove they have a better
  offer from a competitor.

- **Getting the salesperson to make the first offer.**
  "You'll have to do better" is a statement often used
  by the prospect to get the salesperson to state a
  position. Falling into the trap, most salespeople will
  suggest an alternative, such as a 5% price reduction.
  Having made that "offer" now becomes the best
  price you will ever realize on this deal, and often
  the negotiation starts from this new level. This is
  bad news for the salesperson.

- **Splitting the difference.** If the prospect is
  successful in getting the salesperson to make the
  first offer, and then counters that offer with
  something lower ("I was thinking10%, not 5%"),
  splitting the difference can seem like a "fair" way to
  resolve the issue, and offers the prospect of getting
  the deal done without further negotiation. The
  problem is that the deal will be done on the
  prospect's terms, not yours.

- **The flinch**. This maneuver strikes fear in the heart of most salespeople, putting them on the defensive immediately, and giving the prospect the advantage. It's such a simple move. If you're not familiar with it, here's how it plays out. When the salesperson quotes the price to the prospect, the prospect immediately responds by saying, "Wow, that's a lot more than I thought it would be," or words to that effect. Accompanying the words with the appropriate body language and tonality, the message to the seller is clear – lower your price or this will be over quickly. Almost reflexively, sellers respond with some sort of price concession in an effort to stay in the game.

These tactics can be viewed as manipulation on the part of the prospect, but no one said it had to be a fair fight. Recognize it for what it is and deal with it. Remember, knowledge is power. By the way, you can use the very same tactics on the buyer; you just have to be proactive and use them first.

Preparing for a Negotiation

Do your research. Know as much information about the company your negotiating with as well as the individuals involved in the process. Information is power. Know what's at stake for all parties:
- The company's goals, pressures, options during negotiations
- The negotiators' personal goals, pressures, options
- Their bottom line.
- What will happen if they decide to walk away from the negotiations?
- What are they willing to concede?

Know your position. Why are you involved in the negotiations and what do expect to achieve? Be absolutely certain what your stance would be in the following scenarios:

- **Best-case scenario:** What does your ideal outcome look like? Is it acceptable to the other parties involved? This may be a pipedream, but you could also get lucky.
- **Worst-case scenario:** What is the worst possible circumstance in which you will still sign the deal and do business? In other words, what is your bottom line?
- **Anticipated/expected scenario:** What is the most probable result? What conditions/concessions might be involved to achieve this result?
- **Break point:** At what point will you get up and leave negotiations? This point is important because it distinguishes what is a good deal vs. a bad deal for your organization. It is an absolute limit on what you're willing to accept as a reasonable deal.
- **Back up plan:** What's your alternative to signing a deal? What will you do if you can't reach an agreement? Having a back up plan is a powerful mechanism that will alleviate the pressure to make a deal.

The Fundamentals

1. **Set the tone of the negotiation by speaking first.** Use a meeting agreement to set the structure for the meeting. The meeting agreement should include the time set for the meeting; the agenda for the meeting and outcome that we want to manage the meeting to. "When we're through today, what would be a great result for you?" would be a good question to ask.

2. **By asking the most questions, you'll determine the content and direction of the negotiation.** You control the negotiation by asking questions and listening, not by monopolizing the conversation. Try to get the prospect to complete a shopping list of his personal and organizational needs and understand exactly what he wants. You must remember that information is power.

3. **Don't argue.** Even when you believe you are right, it's not appropriate to argue with the other players. An argument will hurt any rapport you might have developed and sow the seeds for failure. Negotiating successfully depends on a collaborative effort to share information, not on trying to prove who is right or wrong.

4. **People are "in it" for themselves, not for you.** When preparing for a negotiation, most people only focus on their own needs. But if you know the other side's needs and intentions, you'll have an upper hand in negotiations and will probably walk out with a better deal. You're not prepared to negotiate until you thoroughly understand the other side's motives for negotiations. Find out why they're "in it."

The Art of Making Concessions

We should be trying to create a win/win outcome in every negotiation in order to insure a strong and lasting business relationship. While concessions are an essential element in any negotiation, they can be a threat to maintaining your credibility. The following suggestions will help you improve your results when concessions are necessary.

- **Make a list of value items.** Prior to the negotiation, identify and list the important items/issues for the other party but which have little value to you. Likewise, make a list of items/services that you want in return (these may be both valuable or small concessions for the other party). Use these items when concessions are brought up. Be prepared!

- **Never respond immediately to a request for a concession.** Take your time. A pause will add uncertainty to the other party, it will add value to the concession if you do make it and you will have more time to think about a comparable concession to request. All of this raises your credibility.

- **Never make a concession without asking for one in return.** As previously mentioned, making unilateral concessions is a big mistake. It sends the wrong message and you lose an opportunity to improve your position. Always ask for something of equal or greater value in return. If you are asked for a concession, you can simply respond, "The only way I could do that is if you could do something for me. I'd need you to _____. How do you feel about that?"

- **Struggle.** Never give up a concession without giving the prospect the impression that they're asking for too much. "A 5% price reduction! That's going to be a tough one. You must think we have a lot of room to spare, but we don't."

- **Beware of "insignificant" concessions.** Small, "insignificant" concessions can add if up if the other party constantly asks for more. Always read their entire proposal before agreeing to a "small" concession. This gives you more power/credibility and provides chances to ask for more concessions from their side. If this becomes an issue, call them on it: "In addition to that, are there other items that you're interested in?" This forces the other party to reveal all of their wishes at once so that they don't continue to peck away at you with more requests.

- **Try to design a system for making concessions.** When necessary, such as negotiating with someone who wants to play hardball, set the tone and the ground rules up front so there is no miscommunication. An easy approach would be to say, "You give me a concession, and I'll give you one." This is an honored technique that's been used cross-culturally for thousands of years and can be used today with anyone in almost any negotiation.

- **Never say never.** By saying "no" or "we can't do that," you limit your own options. Instead, consider saying to the other party, "Hmmm...that may be difficult for us. Can you think of any possible alternatives you may want to consider?" or, "It's a possibility if you can do _____ for us." To use this approach effectively, you must know your list of value items well.

- **Don't ask for unreasonable concessions.** You want to reach a final agreement by finding mutually agreeable items for both sides. Therefore, don't ask for concessions you don't believe you will get. Also, be prudent with any offer because the other party may accept it.

- **Know your business' needs and bottom line.** Never give something away or work for a concession if it doesn't make sense for your business.

- **The "value" of price.** Price is seldom the real issue. The conviction that a person has that he is receiving overall value in the deal is usually the true issue. Consequently, a good deal results from the belief that the person is receiving a good deal.

- **Make sure the other party walks away feeling like a winner.** If the other negotiator can go back to their company and say, "This is what I won for us from the deal," he will feel like he succeeded. Successful negotiators with a win/win philosophy can make this look easy.

Key Negotiating Tactics

There are a handful of Common Sense Selling® tactics that are especially useful when you are in a negotiating environment.

- **Meeting Agreements.** Try to set the tempo yourself, including time and mutual objectives. Agree that it's sometimes okay not to reach agreement and to simply dissolve negotiations if there's no mutually agreeable outcome.
- **Reward & Refocus.** It's important to keep the prospect talking. "Thanks for sharing your concerns about our warranty. How do you think we could resolve that?"
- **Let's Pretend.** Present a hypothetical situation and ask the prospect what he would do. "Let's pretend we could agree to that, what would happen then?"
- **Takeaway.** "It doesn't appear that we may be able to get this done. What do you think?"
- **The Scale.** Using this rating system will help you understand the prospect's priorities and commitment. "On a scale of 1-10, with 10 being a done deal, how close are we?"
- **Landmines.** Deal with anticipated problems early in the negotiation. "My biggest concern is that you'd be willing to make a deal even if it wasn't a good one for me."
- **Divide & Conquer.** When they ask for a concession, see if there's anything else you'll have to give up. "You're asking me to give you an additional 30 days to pay for the product. Is there

anything else you want before I deal with payment terms or is that it?"

Being a skilled negotiator can mean the difference between getting the business or not. Just as important, it can mean the difference in getting the business on your terms or theirs. Prepare well for every situation that might require some sort of negotiation and try to manage the situation so that both parties felt like they have been treated fairly and received a deal that is good for them. Finally, know when to walk away.

<u>Key Points</u>
1. Preparation is the key to negotiating successfully. Know your value items and position. Information is power.
2. Be prepared to walk away if necessary. Know your alternatives.
3. Both parties should come out winners.

Chapter 19
Prospecting

Most sales managers we speak with express frustration that their salespeople are not in front of enough qualified prospects. This seems to be the number one issue that companies have. The ability of the sales force to keep the pipeline full is key to success. Without an effective prospecting system in place, the sales pipeline is weak, creating pressure to be more aggressive in selling to less qualified prospects. This leads to poor sales and margins, frustrated salespeople and concerned management.

Why Salespeople Don't Prospect

Prospecting is an activity that is filled with rejection. You've got to deal with gatekeepers, people claiming they're happy with their existing supplier, they're too busy to see you, etc.

CALL AVOIDANCE

The bottom line is that you represent, in their minds, someone who simply needs to generate more business for your company and they don't see much value in meeting with you so that you can attempt to "sell" them. Every day they have to deal with salespeople who want a piece of their time, and they don't see you as being any different. In some industries salespeople need to make 50-60 cold calls just to get one appointment. With all this rejection, is it any wonder that salespeople look for any excuse not to prospect?

Focusing on the Wrong End of the Problem

Most salespeople focus on the results of their prospecting efforts, and that's a mistake. While results are important, it's impossible for you to control results. You have, for example, no control whether or not the person you are calling is in, and if he is, whether or not he'll take your call or agree to meet with you. Most salespeople become frustrated and their attitude becomes negative when their results are not as productive as they'd like. They worry about things they can't control, and even take it as a personal failure. Does that make sense? Our advice is simple – don't worry about what you can't control.

Instead, focus on those things that you can control. For example, you can control your own behavior - the activities that you do. If you set prospecting goals for yourself, such as making ten cold calls per day, every day that you make those ten calls is a successful prospecting day. If you do the behavior, you will get results.

This bears repeating because it can change your entire attitude toward prospecting, create more sales opportunities for you and increase your sales. Don't beat yourself up because you didn't get the appointment or the sale. Focus on what you can control; focus on your plan and executing it. If your plan includes cold calls, decide how many dials you need to make every day and make them. Then you've had a successful day, every day. Try that and see what happens to your attitude about prospecting, and your results.

Prospecting is a Discarding Activity

You'll remember the California gold prospectors back in the middle of the 1800's. Panning for gold in the streams and rivers of Northern California was a tedious activity. It was definitely hard work, but the rewards were great for those who persevered. They might have to sift through hundreds or thousands of pans of gravel just to find one small gold nugget. If they became discouraged every time a pan of gravel yielded only rocks and sand, they wouldn't have lasted long, and certainly some didn't. If you become discouraged every time a prospecting call comes up empty, you won't last long either.

Try changing your attitude. Think of prospecting as a discarding activity. You're discarding those who are not prospects, and each time you discard one you get closer to that gold nugget. Let's face it, prospecting is a head game in many ways, so get your head straight if you want to win the game.

Don't Put All Your Eggs in One Prospecting Basket

Most successful prospectors have more than one method of prospecting. They don't put all their eggs in one basket. Here are a few proven ways to find prospects, but every business is different and some of these activities may or may not fit for you. Select several that fit your model.

- Prospecting within your current accounts for expanded business where you have an established relationship.
- Referral prospecting where you use your current customer base to refer you to others.

- Networking at professional meetings, association meetings and anywhere else that your prospects or good referring sources may gather.
- Sponsoring small-scale seminars where you can be the subject matter expert.
- Direct mail or email for lead generation.
- Print, TV or radio advertising in appropriate markets.
- Participation at trade shows or special exhibits.
- Publicity and other forms of public relations.
- Newsletters, both in print and email.
- Community and civic involvement.
- "How to" articles in client-orientated publications.
- Speeches at client industry meetings.
- Cold calling.

Your Prospecting Message – Don't Blow It

Once you've gained the attention of that hard to reach prospect, you'd better make sure that your initial message moves you forward, not backward. This is where most salespeople blow it. Given the chance to make a great first impression and set themselves apart from the competition, they do just the opposite. It's an opportunity wasted.

The Traditional Elevator Speech

The "Elevator Speech" is a short commercial that tells a prospect about the company and it's products or services. Typically it's designed to create interest and make the company sound like the best thing since sliced bread. It's loaded with feature and benefit statements, such as:
- "We're a leader in our field"
- "We have a long list of very satisfied clients"
- "We can save you time and money"

- "We can help you solve your problems"

We might be tempted to assume that that's exactly what everyone is looking for, but unfortunately, it's the same pitch everyone is making. For that reason it makes you look like your competitors, has the effect of making you a "commodity" in the eyes of your prospect and does little to create the credibility you are seeking. Furthermore, it telegraphs that you're a salesperson, causing the prospect to become defensive. That's why the traditional elevator speech doesn't work. In essence, it's what we call "salesperson's disease," a premature presentation and usually ends up with a premature rejection. If anybody has ever said "no" to you when you know that under the right circumstances you might be the best thing for their company, then you've experienced premature rejection.

The typical elevator speech is totally focused on the company and it's products and does nothing to help begin to qualify the prospect. It often concludes with the prospect saying something like this, "Why don't you just send me some literature first." How many times have you heard that one? You need to get the prospect to start talking immediately, getting the focus on their problems and the things that are important to them.

People Buy for Their Reasons

Unless your prospect has a problem that you can fix, he's not really a prospect, as we've discussed in other sections of this book. Trying to create interest with your features and benefits is a low percentage play, yet that's the objective of the traditional elevator speech.

Typically, salespeople assume that everyone who has the characteristics of someone they've done business with in the past is a prospect. This is simply not so and is a fatal mistake that many salespeople make. Have you ever tried to sell someone who was completely happy with your competitor? If so, you know that getting them to switch is typically a long, difficult process and that often you need to cut price drastically to get any interest at all. A real prospect is someone who has a problem and is committed to fixing it. Furthermore, they must have the financial resources to fix it, have the authority to make a decision and be willing to make that decision in a time frame that is comfortable for both parties.

The hierarchy of motivation, as we've discussed, is...

- Pain - you're in trouble and you want to get out of it
- Fear - you see trouble coming and you want to avoid it
- Gain – things are good, but could be better
- Interest – curiosity

Feature and benefit statements are designed to create interest, but that's the lowest level of motivation. We're aiming at the wrong target.

Obviously, the secret is to understand the prospect's issues/pain (if they have any) before we try to get them to understand how our products and services might help them. Forget the features and benefits when you're trying to find out if you have a prospect. You'll be able to use them in your presentation later, assuming you have a prospect that qualifies for a presentation.

Getting the Prospect to Divulge His Pain

By now you're wondering how you get the prospect to open up and divulge the pain on a cold call, since prospects typically have their guard up when dealing with salespeople. It's really quite simple, but it breaks every traditional rule of selling.

The first step is to tell the prospect early on that it's okay for him to say "no" to you if there's not a fit. Act like you are a successful sales professional and have a full pipeline.

Telling a prospect that "no" is an acceptable response serves two purposes. First, it is a statement that makes the prospect feel less threatened. When a prospect knows the salesperson will accept "no" for an answer, he can relax. When he relaxes he will open up and talk with you honestly. Second, it's an attitude that you, the salesperson, must have. When you get comfortable hearing "no" and realize that it is an acceptable part of the game, your attitude will change positively. Let's face it, not everyone is a prospect. The sooner you can determine that they are not a prospect the more efficient you will be.

The more effective you become at qualifying the prospect, the more you will enjoy the unique experience of having the prospect convince you that he has a problem and is looking for a solution. But until you learn how to qualify more effectively, just adopt the following attitude:

***It's the prospect's job to convince me that
he has a problem and is serious about solving it.***

When this becomes your philosophy, you'll find yourself behaving differently on every sales call. You'll ask more questions, better questions and, executed properly, the prospect will either "sell" you or you will move on to someone who is a better prospect.

If your pipeline was really full and you didn't need the business, would you conduct yourself differently on a cold call? Would you "beg" for an appointment, seem desperate to get the order? Make presentations all over the place? Of course not. Okay, so your pipeline isn't full. Just fake it until you make it and see what a difference it makes. (Please note that this is not intended to come across as arrogance - simply confidence and strength.) This attitude will help you execute the prospecting tactics that we'll discuss shortly.

The Elevator Speech / Introductory Pain Probe

The Elevator Speech is the tactic you will use to quickly determine whether or not the prospect has a problem your products and services might solve. It's our initial qualifying question. Don't make it any more complicated than that.

Bring in some of your best customers and ask them what the top three or four reasons were that they bought your product. Ask them what they were sick and tired of, what were they angry about and what frustrated them that caused them to explore and purchase your solution. Listen very carefully to their responses and take a lot of notes. You will start to hear real "pains" and at different levels of the organization the "pains" will be different.

They might be saying things like...

- "We're really concerned about the amount of money we were spending on ......"
- "We're frustrated with our vendor's inability to handle warranty claims in a timely manner."
- "We're sick and tired of the network going down so frequently."
- "We're upset about the constant backorder situation."
- "We're angry because we haven't made our sales goals in the last three quarters."

Make a long list of these pains. At different levels of the organization the pains will probably be different, so your Elevator Speech will need to be modified for your audience. These pains can be inserted into your Elevator Speech.

Building Your Elevator Speech

An effective Elevator Speech should contain the following elements:

- Your introduction - your name & company. ("I'm _____ with _____."
- A brief explanation of what your company does (assuming your prospect doesn't know). ("We're a ...")
- A short statement about why you are unique (assuming you <u>do</u> have something that is unique such as a proprietary process for doing something – don't say things like great service or dedicated people since any competitor can make that claim). ("What's unique about us is ...")
- A description of your typical client. ("We work with...")
- A short pain menu (2-3 issues) about why people use your company. ("Usually people come to us because they are frustrated because...or concerned about...")
- A probe for the prospect's pain. ("Before I go any further, are any of these situations that you're dealing with?")

The Prospect's Response

Notice that your Elevator Speech ends with a question... "Are any of these issues for you?" Now you wait for a response. There are only <u>two</u> possible responses that your prospect can have:

- "Yes, everybody's got those issues." Then you'd say, "If you had to pick one, which is the most important?" After the prospect picked one, you would say, "Tell me a little more about that; why was that one important?
- The prospect could say, "No, everything's fine." Then you would say, "Well, if there was one thing that could be improved, what would it be?" If they mentioned something, you'd say, "Tell me more."

If they had no pains, you would say, "Thanks for your time, glad things are going so well. Good bye." Simply hang up and make another call.

The Traditional v. The New Elevator Speech

So that you can see the difference, here are examples of the old versus the new. Maybe the old elevator speech doesn't sound exactly like yours, but we've heard responses similar to these hundreds of times when we've asked questions like, "who are you," "what's this about" or "tell me about your company."

The Old Pitch
The call starts with, *"I'm Bob with XYZ Printing. How are you today?"*

The "clever" segue into the sales pitch, assuming we still have the prospect on the line, goes something like this. *"We're the premier printing company in the area. We've been serving the local market for over 20 years and have the most advanced digital printing equipment in the area. Our specialty is quick turnaround and competitive pricing. I'd like to set an appointment to meet with you to show you how we can save you time and money on your next printing project. Would Tuesday afternoon or Wednesday morning be better for you?"*

Does that sound familiar? It probably does and there are many problems with this approach:

- *"How are you today?"* Every telemarketer in the world starts the call by asking about the prospect's "well-being." While this is an honest attempt at politeness, prospects know you don't really care, so it comes across as insincere and makes you sound like a telemarketer.

159

- The "compelling" pitch by the printing salesperson sounds like the other printing company that called the prospect yesterday. They said they were the best in town and could save him time and money too. Whom should he believe?
- *"Tuesday afternoon or Wednesday morning?"* How many times have we heard that over used alternative choice close? Nearly every salesperson (over)uses it.
- The salesperson wants an appointment but doesn't want to take the time to find out if there's any pain. This is the typical product pusher's strategy and the prospect knows it.
- The easy blow off that the prospect can, and often does, use is to say, "Just send me some information about it." And you know how sincere that request is.

The New Elevator Speech Using the CSS Cold Call Script

This call starts with, *"I'm Bob Smith with XZY Printing. Did I get you at a bad time?"*

If you get permission to continue, you'd say, *"Thanks for taking my call. Can I take about 20 seconds to tell you why I called, then you can tell me if we need to talk further?"*

When you get permission, you'd say, *"I'll be brief, right to the point. We're one of the leading commercial printing companies in the area. Typically companies switch to us because they're upset with long turnaround times, concerned about the inconsistent quality of the final product or frustrated that their printer can't offer any creative ideas to improve the job. Are any of these issues for you?"*

160

If the answer is affirmative, you'd explore the pain further, starting with, *"Not unusual, can you tell me a little more about that?"*

If the answer is negative, you could conclude the call quickly by saying, *"Sorry to have bothered you. Have a good day."* And make another call. Remember, you're trying to find that gold nugget quickly and not waste time with people who are not good prospects.

The benefits to this approach are many:

- Asking if you got him at a bad time is respectful of the prospect's time. (The overwhelming majority of the people we train say this tactic has been very effective despite the initial concern about making it too easy for him to say that he is busy.)
- The "pitch" focuses on possible problems your company can address, thus begins the qualifying process quickly.
- It's different.
- You won't have done anything to destroy rapport.
- You won't sound like every other salesperson that calls.

The Many Uses of the Elevator Speech

The Elevator Speech can be used at the beginning of any meeting with a prospective client. This includes cold calls, but also works well at trade shows, networking events and anyplace when you're talking to someone who may be a prospect. It helps refocus the meeting from you and your company to the prospect and his pains. It's an important tool for you to master.

<u>Key Points</u>

1. The only way you can fail at prospecting is if you don't prospect.

2. The only thing you can completely control is your own activity (dialing the phone), so that is where your focus must be.
3. Your prospecting activities today will determine your sales success tomorrow.
4. If there's no "pain," don't expect to get an appointment.

Chapter 20
Referral Prospecting

Referrals are the best way to increase your sales. When you begin to build your business through referrals you will lessen your dependence on having to make cold calls and other less productive (and frustrating) prospecting activities. Yet getting qualified referrals is not automatic, by any stretch of the imagination. There is a prerequisite.

The most important concept to understand about referrals is that you must provide outstanding service, superior products and be professional in every way in order for anyone to consider providing you with referrals. No one will want to refer friends and business associates to you if they are concerned that their referral might have a bad experience with you or your products. Until you have achieved those standards, referrals will not be a major source of business for you.

Having said that, the vast majority of professional salespeople who do provide outstanding service and quality products still do not get nearly the number or quality of referrals that they should, missing out on the easiest way to build their business. As a result they work too hard, have to resort to other, less productive, forms of prospecting and their business and income suffers.

Why Don't Salespeople Get Referrals?

If referrals are the easiest way to build business, why don't salespeople get more referrals? It's not always due to the lack of quality or professional standards, but rather other factors, and this chapter will address them all.

1. They don't ask for them
2. They don't know how to ask for referrals
3. They don't tell the referring source what they're looking for

Our experience is that most salespeople don't know how to ask for referrals and as a result, when they do they hear things from the potential referring source like, "I can't think of anybody right now, but if I do, I'll call you." And as if to reinforce their commitment to providing you with future referrals, they ask for "a few of your business cards" to give out. (Sure, that's going to happen.) But the negative reinforcement in this example is key. The more often this type of thing happens, the more we start to believe that asking for referrals is futile. And if we believe it's futile, pretty soon we stop asking.

Often salespeople see having to ask for referrals as a "begging" activity. They believe that if they were really successful they wouldn't even have to ask for referrals - they'd have all the business they could handle. Clearly the superstar attitude causes problems.

When someone asks you for a referral, what is your typical response? If you normally say, "I can't think of anybody right now, but if I do...," then you are very susceptible to having what might be called "referral avoidance empathy" – a belief that your client feels the same way you do. Then your subconscious thought process goes something like this: I normally don't give referrals myself and suspect that he doesn't either, so why bother asking? If that's what you're thinking, you're done; it's over. No referrals for you.

There's a lot we could say about referrals, but simply understanding the following will help you improve your referral business by 100%.

When to Ask

The best time to ask for referrals certainly depends on a lot of factors. But here are a few ideas.

- Set the stage early in the relationship. ("At some point when you're totally satisfied with us as a supplier, I'd like to ask you for referrals. How do you feel about that?")
- After you've just completed delivery of your solution and your customer is satisfied. ("Who do you know…?")
- After you've just received the order.
- Anytime you get in front of someone, even if they haven't bought.

Dos and Don'ts

- Ask them about their willingness to give you referrals. Don't assume they will.
- Begin the question with "Who do you know that................?" Don't ask, "Do you know anyone ....?." It's too easy for them to say, "I can't think of anyone right now, but if I do......"
- Ask to be <u>introduced</u> to their friends and associates. Don't ask to be <u>recommended</u> - it puts too much pressure on the prospect and is presumptive.
- Focus your question on the end result to the client - a benefit or problem you can solve.
- Phrase the question as though the referring source will be doing the friend a favor.
- Tell your referring source exactly what you will be doing with the referral. Don't forget to keep the referring source informed of your progress.

How to Ask for a Referral

Knowing what to say is half the battle. First, qualify for their interest in referring people to you. Here are some ways to do that.

- "How do you feel about referring to me?"

- "How do you feel about helping people you know with similar problems?"
- "How do you feel about helping me grow my business?"
- "How do you feel about helping me tell my story to people who might have an interest in what I do?"
- "I want to build my business through referrals. I have a goal for the quarter to secure ten new clients through referrals. If I can help you so it takes very little time and you are confident that I will represent you well, would you be willing to help me?"
- "My job is finding qualified people to whom I can tell my story. I think you can help me do this. Would you be willing to help me?"
- "Basically, I get paid in two ways. I get paid when you like the work I've done and we do business together. The other way I get paid is when you like the work I've done and you refer me to your friends and business associates. How do you feel about that?"
- "In my business most people spend 80% of their time selling and only 20% on servicing existing clients like yourself. My objective is to reverse that ratio and spend the majority of my time taking care of my customers. That leaves very little time to develop new business, so I'm asking for your assistance in that area by providing me with referrals. That way I can continue to spend most of my time taking care of your needs. How do you feel about referring people to me?"

Asking "who do you know…?" (an open-ended question) as opposed to "do you know anyone …" (closed-end question) is a far more effective way to get referrals.

Here are a few options.

- "Who do you know who might need my product or service?"
- "Who do you know that has plans for the future that require what I do?"
- "Who do you know that is facing the same kinds of challenges that you are?"
- "Who do you know that may be a good Center of Influence for me?"
- "Do you know who is in charge of _____ at _____? Would you call him/her on my behalf?"

Here's a novel way to open up a dialogue on referrals. It's especially helpful when you haven't been proactive yourself. It might seem like you're putting a guilt trip on the referring source, and works best on people with whom you have a very good relationship.

- "I haven't received any referrals from you in some time now. Usually when that happens it's because you're not completely satisfied with our service. I hope that's not the case here."

Sometimes building a referral team is a good strategy. This involves working with another salesperson that serves a similar market that you do.

- "There may be clients that you have that we can serve together, and vice versa. Let's set up a time to explore how we can work as a team, and perhaps even look at bringing in other professionals to strengthen the resources we can offer our clients. By working together and referring to one another, we can build our businesses through our efforts to better serve our clients."
- "I need your help. Based on your influence in the community (or industry, etc.) I would like you to become a Center of Influence for me. Here's what a

Center of Influence is...................... Here's the kind of thing I would like you to do for me........................ And here's what I will do for you in return."

Your Ideal Client Profile

Salespeople will experience more success if they can be specific when asking people for referrals. After all, it's easier for the referring source if you can take the guesswork out of referrals. If you can clearly describe the type of person or company you are looking for, your referring source will find it easier to focus on someone that fits your ideal profile. This will result in better quality referrals, and more of them.

Take a moment to develop your ideal client profile. Here are some ideas about what to include.

- Description: (ex. an owner of a small to medium sized business who has a sales force; VP of Sales larger company)
- Typical Pains: (ex. who is frustrated with excessive turnover, not making his/her sales goals, etc.)
- Mindset: (ex. open minded about training; deadly serious about growing the business.)
- Geographic: (ex. located in …)
- Products & Services: (ex. is used to going outside the company for sales training)
- Profit/Purchase Potential:
- Other Factors:

"Upgrade" Your Referrals

So far we've spent a great deal of time on how to ask for referrals. But this is only half the battle, as you'll see.

Most salespeople are quite happy to get a name and a number to call. They thank the referring source and then start the process of <u>making a cold call</u> on the (often unsuspecting) referral. This is usually a frustrating process that yields poor results.

A better way is to "upgrade" your referrals, like this. When you get a referral from someone, do the following:

- Probe for pain: "What problems do they have that you think I could help them with?"
- Solicit their help: "Would you feel comfortable calling him to see if he wants to speak with me?" (Let the referring source make the cold call for you.)
- Try for an introduction: "What would you think about the three of us having lunch one day. I'll buy." (If you can get a personal introduction, the referring source will be your best advocate and will do much of the selling for you.)

Get as far as you can in upgrading your referrals. Simply getting only a name and a number will give you less than a 5% conversion rate, while an introduction will be 50% or higher.

Finally, Give More to Get More

Referring should not be a one-sided activity. The more referrals you give, the more you will get. There should always be something in it for your referring source.

- Try to provide them with referrals in return. Make a point of asking your clients whom they would like to be introduced to and see if you can help them.
- You can make them look good if product/service benefits referral.
- You might provide a reward such as lunch or small token of appreciation.
- You could pay a referral fee (if their company has no policy against it).
- They'll feel good about helping someone.

Key Points
1. If you don't ask for referrals, you usually don't get them.
2. The more referrals you give, the more you will receive.
3. Don't let them guess about whom you'd like to do business with.
4. The only way you'll get referred is if you are exceeding their expectations.

Chapter 21
Pre-Call Preparation

Now that you're familiar with Common Sense Selling®, you have one of the most important tools any salesperson can have, a proven sales process. The last chapter in this book addresses the first thing the successful salesperson should do before he can implement his sales process – call preparation.

The lesson is clear - effective preparation is the key to success. While this seems obvious, many salespeople simply hop in their car and drive off to the appointment with little or no significant preparation. Their attitude is that one sales call is like any other. They are winging it, leaving things to chance, which is always a poor strategy.

All of us have experienced that empty feeling of nervousness when we're not prepared. Proper preparation will help build your confidence with the knowledge that you are ready for any eventuality, and that confidence will come across to your prospect. You'll look more professional than your competition, giving you an early advantage. Your questions will be more focused, more relevant to the prospect's situation. Since first impressions are so important, being properly prepared can get you out of the gate in front of the pack.

The 5 P's

    Proper

        Preparation

            Prevents

                Poor

                    Performance

Everyone has his or her own method of preparing for a sales call. Undoubtedly, you are already doing some of the things mentioned here. Our preparation focuses on four critical areas: research, introspection, communication and rehearsal. Let's look at each.

Research

A week or two before your first meeting take some time to find out as much as you can about your prospect's industry, the company and it's key people (with a focus on those you will be dealing with). The Internet is a great resource, providing a wealth of information, such as:

- Company websites, which include executive profiles, press releases, financial information, products and services offered, company business philosophy, customers, etc. Print important pages and keep them in your file.
- Do a search for industry associations to find out trends and other relevant information.
- First Research (www.firstresearch.com) is a web-based subscription service that provides information on a wide variety of companies.
- For publicly traded companies, Earnings.com is a good resource.
- Most good size cities have a local Business Journal weekly newspaper. Information on smaller local companies can often be found at www.bizjournals.com, a website that represents nation's largest publisher of metropolitan business newspapers, serving 41 of the country's most vibrant markets

Additional sources of information include:
- Company sales departments
- D&B reports
- Your local Chamber of Commerce

- Your company's internal database and other company salespeople who may have experience with the company
- Existing customers who may know the company
- Your referring source (assuming you were referred in)
- Other local newspapers and business publications

Don't forget competition. The properly prepared salesperson will constantly be looking for information about his competitors. Understanding their strengths and weaknesses and how they have responded to competitive situations in the past can be critical when strategizing how you will attempt to sell a prospect.

Introspection

After you've done the bulk of your research, it's time to start planning your strategy for the first call. At the very least, this planning should include the following:

- **Primary objectives.** This should answer the question: "If this was a great sales call, the following objectives would have been achieved."
- **Secondary objectives.** Often we don't, for whatever reason, achieve our primary objectives. Your secondary objectives would define what a successful call would be in the event that your primary objectives were not met.
- **Specific information to obtain.** Don't forget that one of your primary objectives on your first call is to qualify the prospect. Make a list of the things you need to find out to determine if you have a real opportunity that you should invest time in.
- **Anticipated roadblocks.** Problems can be dealt with more successfully if you are prepared. Roadblocks you might encounter could include a

long-standing relationship with their vendor or lack of access to the ultimate decision-maker. Develop a strategy for dealing with them if they arise.

- **Information (company marketing literature) to take.** The meeting, if properly set up, should focus on the prospect and the critical business issues he wants to address. Therefore, the more material you bring the more the focus will be on you. Consider taking nothing except something to take notes on.
- **Third party stories.** You may be asked about other companies you have worked with that have the same pain issues as your prospect. Be prepared to respond with anecdotes about these clients and the products and services that you delivered to assist them. Find out if you can use these clients as references if you are asked.

You might consider developing a worksheet that includes the above items to use for call planning purposes.

Communication

Communication is critical to a successful relationship. Insuring that both you and your prospect are on the same page eliminates surprises and builds trust. When you made the appointment you should have set a good meeting agreement, covering the time allotted for the meeting, the meeting objectives (for both parties) and what would happen at the end of the meeting (agree on next steps or close the file). Consider sending an email to confirm the meeting and the agenda.

Calling a day or two before the appointment to confirm is optional. One theory is that it gives the prospect an opportunity to back out of the appointment. Personally, we only call to confirm if we have to travel a significant distance (over 50 miles) and want to avoid the possibility of being stood up, or if the prospect asks me to call to confirm. Otherwise we assume the prospect will respect my time and honor the appointment. We've had very few disappointments over the years.

Rehearsal

On the day of the meeting make sure you have directions to your prospect's place of business, and leave with plenty of time to spare so you don't have to stress out about possible traffic delays or becoming lost. If you can eliminate this cause of stress, you will arrive with a more positive mindset, which is key to having a successful meeting. Arriving 10-15 minutes early gives you time to relax and continue your preparation, which should include the following:

- Reviewing your objectives for the meeting
- Rehearsing your meeting agreement
- Reviewing the questions that you will ask (review Whetstone's Pocket Coach)
- Mentally envisioning yourself having a successful meeting

No doubt you're thinking that this is a lot of preparation. It is. But, it's virtually impossible to over-prepare for a sales meeting with a prospect. A good rule of thumb is – the bigger the opportunity, the more preparation is required.

One final thought - preparation is important for every meeting, not just the first one with a new prospect.

Key Points
1. Remember the **5 P's** - **P**roper **P**reparation **P**revents **P**oor **P**erformance.
2. Research shows that the best-prepared salespeople are the most successful.
3. You can't be too prepared.

Chapter 22
The Ideal Sale –
Putting Common Sense Selling®
Into Practice

Introduction

This narrative, though abbreviated, shows how a salesperson might implement the Common Sense Selling® process in a fictitious, yet realistic, sales opportunity. It attempts to answer the question, "How would a salesperson use the Common Sense Selling® process in a sales opportunity in the 'real' world?"

I've attempted to focus on the most important aspects of Common Sense Selling®; the initial call and qualifying the prospect. While it might seem that this sales cycle is just a few weeks long, in reality you might need more or less time to get the business closed. Obviously I'm taking some poetic license in order to make the points that I think are important for you to understand. You'll no doubt be thinking, "It's not that easy," and I understand that. My sales opportunities sometimes aren't this easy either. Remember, this is fiction, but based on fact. Use it as a tool for learning.

After much deliberation, I've also decided to use "widgets" as the product or service. And I know that you don't sell widgets, but if I had used printing services, or software, or copiers, or something else, I'd have excluded 99% of the readers anyway. So it's widgets for this example. You can substitute your product or service every time you read widgets and you'll probably be right on the money.

Here goes.

The Seller – Steve Watson of Pacific Widget

Steve Watson was a sales rep with Pacific Widget, a mid-sized regional widget manufacturer in California. Pacific had a respectable 25% share of the widget market in the western states. Steve had nearly ten years sales experience in the widget business, and had consistently been one of the top producers for Pacific Widget. Steve had been through sales training in the Common Sense Selling® methodology several years before and had enthusiastically adopted it in his selling efforts.

Unfortunately, Steve was currently facing a selling challenge of considerable proportions. Recently one of his major clients had recently merged with an east coast company and he needed to replace the loss of about a million dollars of profitable business annually.

The Prospect – Solana Manufacturing

As Steve looked over his options, Solana Manufacturing appeared on the radar screen. Solana was a long time customer of Delta Widget, one of Pacific's stronger competitors. Over the years Solana had seemingly been "married" to Delta Widget, and had never given Steve much of an opportunity to create a serious dialogue with them. However, Solana had recently installed a new management team, and Steve calculated that this might be the opening he was looking for.

Mike Curtis was Solana's new CEO. He had been recruited about six months before when Solana had missed their aggressive forecasts for the second straight year. Mike had brought in several key people, including a new VP of Operations. Mike was a no nonsense business person with a strong desire to see Solana pass the 100 million dollar mark in sales in the next two years. Sales were currently in the $75 million range. Solana had used

Delta exclusively as their widget supplier for the past five years, and widgets were a major element in their manufacturing process, with annual purchases in the five million dollar range.

The other key players from Solana were Nancy Martin, Solana's new VP of Operations and Bruce McCall, the Director of Purchasing. Bruce reported to Nancy.

The Competition – Delta Widget

Delta Widget was one of Pacific's strongest competitors, but recently been acquired by Consolidated General, a large conglomerate based in New York. While the ramifications of the acquisition had yet to be totally sorted out, there had been reports that some of the changes had resulted in some supply and service problems. Additionally, Delta's rep who had called on Solana for years had seen the acquisition as a good opportunity to take early retirement.

Initiating the Sales Process - The Cold Call

Steve called Sandy, Mike's administrative assistant, and explained the nature of his call. Rather than trying to get "past" Sandy, as so many people suggested he do, his tactic was to see if Sandy could help him secure an appointment with Mike.

Sandy answered the phone with, "Good morning. Mike Curtis' office. This is Sandy. May I help you?" Mike knew that this was his first chance to make a good impression and he didn't want to sound like every other salesperson that was trying to get an appointment with Mike. He was feeling the pressure.

He said, "Good morning, Sandy, this is Steve Watson with Pacific Widget. Can I have a moment of your time?" Sandy thought to herself. Well, this is another sales guy, but he sounds different. He didn't just ask to be put through to Mike. She replied, "Sure, what's it about?"

178

"I need your help," answered Steve. "I'm trying to get some time on Mike's calendar to discuss Pacific Widget's capabilities in light of Delta's recent acquisition by Consolidated General. I don't know if Solana is having any issues as a result of the change, and if you're not, my conversation with Mike will probably be a short one. I'm sure he's a busy guy and I'm looking for some help as to the best way to get on his calendar. Any suggestions?"

Sandy momentarily reflected on a call from another salesperson that she took a few days before. He was pushing pretty hard for an appointment with Mike, she remembered, but was unsuccessful. Mike didn't care much for pushy salespeople, having come up through the sales ranks himself.

"Well, that was refreshing," thought Sandy. "He didn't make any claims like some of the other salespeople who are trying to get on Mike's calendar. I think I'll give him a break." Sandy knew that Mike had expressed frustration with their widget situation recently because of the acquisition and thought he might be willing to speak to Steve. She checked with Mike and recommended he talk to Steve. He agreed, and she put Steve through.

Getting the Appointment with Mike

"Mike, this is Steve Watson with Pacific Widget," he began. "Did I get you at a bad time?"

"I'm always busy. What's it about?" While sounding somewhat gruff, Mike reflected that at least this guy respected his time by asking if it was a good time to talk.

"Mike, let me take about 30 seconds to tell you why I'm calling, then you can tell me if we need to continue. Maybe we won't. I promise to be brief and get right to the point."

"Okay. Go ahead," Mike replied.

"As I said, I'm with Pacific Widget. We're a regional widget supplier based here in Southern California and compete with Delta. With all the changes that have

179

occurred with Delta recently, sometimes we've heard that there have been communication problems and we've also been told that there have been some isolated issues with product and service. But I don't know if any of these are issues for you. Maybe you've been spared those headaches."

"Well, I can tell you that our long time rep, Ken Shea, left shortly after the takeover. I think he took early retirement. He was a great guy and really knew our business well. The new guy...well, I hardly know him. He doesn't have the experience that Ken did and seems to be overwhelmed."

"Interesting," replied Steve. "What kinds of problems is that causing for you?"

Mike responded, "I just don't feel like we always have the support we need. With Delta we've always been a valued customer but I'm not sure that today we can continue to make that statement. We've got some pretty aggressive growth plans for the next couple of years and having a widget supplier that will be a strong partner during this growth is important. The jury's still out on whether I can count on Delta in this area."

"I see. I can understand that could cause some frustration for you," said Steve.

"It is frustrating," said Mike. I don't really know where we stand. You try growing a company like ours without a good widget supplier."

"I can certainly understand that," Steve replied. He continued by saying, "Mike, I said I'd take 30 seconds and I'm over my limit. Can we continue for another couple of minutes or do you have to go?"

"No, it's fine. I've got a few minutes. Thanks for asking." Mike was feeling comfortable with Steve's approach. No pressure, he thought to himself.

Steve continued, "I appreciate that. But I'm curious, when you expressed these concerns about communication and support to the folks at Delta, what did they say?"

"Unfortunately we haven't had much dialogue about it, although we've tried. As I said, the new rep is kind of clueless. He just tells me not to worry about it, that they'll be there when I need them. Quite honestly, I'm not comforted by his remarks. We're starting to explore other options."

Steve sensed that at this point he had heard enough pain from Mike and thought that if he asked for an appointment he'd be successful. "Look, Mike. It would be foolish of me to tell you at this point the we're the answer you're looking for, but would the potential of us being able to address some of these issues be worth the investment of an hour of your time to explore some alternatives?"

"I guess so. Sure. When did you want to come over?" asked Mike. They agreed to meet the following Tuesday at 10:00 am.

Debrief

Steve had spent just a few minutes on the phone with Mike. He was successful in scheduling an appointment, which was his original goal. Some of the things he did that helped him were...

- *Asking Sandy for help, instead of trying to force his way through to Mike.*
- *He asked Mike if it was a good time to talk, realizing that his call was an interruption.*
- *He utilized his Elevator Speech focusing on the kinds of problems that he helped his clients solve instead of doing a feature & benefit "pitch" that would make him sound like every other widget salesperson.*
- *Because he led with "pain statements" instead of features & benefits, the conversation with Mike quickly became focused on the challenges Mike was experiencing as a result of Delta's acquisition by*

Consolidated General. This encouraged Mike to meet with Steve since the dialogue would be focused on his problems, not listening to a sales pitch from another widget supplier.

The last thing to do before hanging up was to set a good Meeting Agreement for the appointment with Mike the following Tuesday morning.

The Opening Meeting Agreement

At the end of the call Steve wanted to make sure he and Mike were both on the same page regarding their expectations for the meeting. Steve also wanted to make sure that Mike would be relaxed enough to talk about his widget needs openly without feeling any pressure. He suspected that several other large widget suppliers had their sights set on Mike's business as well and that the competition would be tough. While they were competitive, Pacific didn't try to get business by offering the lowest prices. He knew he'd have to rely on something other than pricing if he was going to be successful in getting Solana's business. Steve felt that his company was the "best" but knew that his competitors were also very competent suppliers and that he'd need an edge to differentiate himself from the others.

He believed that <u>HOW</u> he sold would be just as important as <u>WHAT</u> he sold. And he knew that he had to set the stage for this differentiation early in his "campaign." The meeting had been set for 10:00 am the following Tuesday. Setting a good meeting agreement on the telephone, Steve knew, was an important element in differentiating himself from the others.

Steve began by asking Mike, "How much time will we have for our meeting next Tuesday, Mike?"

Mike replied, "I've got a fairly busy morning, Steve. Let's try to keep it to an hour. Will that be enough?"

"That would be fine for an initial meeting," Steve said. "And just so we can make sure that our time is well spent, what would be the most important things for us to discuss...from your perspective?"

"I'd like to give you an overview of our current widget situation, and, of course, would like you to give us an overview of what your company can do for us. I'll probably ask Nancy Martin to join us. She's our VP of Operations."

Steve replied, "I was going to ask if anyone else needed to be at the meeting so I'm glad that Nancy will be able to join us. I'm looking forward to meeting her. You know, I'd like to make sure that we set aside some time for me to ask you a few questions. I'm glad to give you a short overview of our capabilities, but it's just as important that I understand what things you're looking to improve. I'm really not coming in to make a presentation; it's just too early for that. Will that be okay?"

Mike acknowledged that they'd be glad to answer any questions that Steve had and Steve continued with the meeting agreement. "Mike, probably what will happen during the meeting is that we'll exchange enough information so that we can decide whether or not we might have a fit...whether or not it makes sense for us to continue our dialogue. And, of course, there's always the possibility that we may not be a fit for one reason or another. If you conclude that we're not, feel free to tell me so. But if it does make sense to continue talking, let's take a minute at the end of the meeting to figure out what our next step should be. Does that sound like a good plan?"

"Sounds good," Mike said.

"Great," said Steve. "I'll see you at 10:00 am next Tuesday. Good bye."

Steve hung up the phone with a feeling of excitement at the prospect of meeting with Mike and his CFO. He felt good because he had set the expectations for the meeting professionally and had tried to remove any pressure that

Mike might be feeling by telling him that it was okay to tell him no if Mike wasn't comfortable talking further. Steve knew that the meeting agreement was key to differentiating him from his competition. He made a mental note to himself that he needed to complete his Pre-Call Planning form so that he was as prepared as he could be for this important meeting with Solana's key managers.

Debrief

Setting a good Opening Meeting Agreement, Steve knew, set the tone for the relationship and, potentially, the entire sales cycle. It helped send a message to Mike that he was different, that he was sincerely interested in understanding and solving Mike's supply challenges and not just trying to make a sale. His Meeting Agreement included several elements and helped in the following ways:

- *Time. Mike agreed to give Steve an hour, indicating that he was sincerely interested in meeting to look at some alternatives.*
- *Solana's Agenda. Mike suggested that he provide Steve an overview of his current supply situation, which would give Steve a great opportunity to ask questions about Mike's concern with his current supplier.*
- *Steve's Purpose. Steve asked for and was given permission to ask questions to better qualify the opportunity.*
- *Next Step. They agreed that at the end of the meeting they'd decide on a specific next step or would agree to "close the file" if Mike did not want to continue. Steve knew that giving Mike the opportunity to say "no" was a powerful tactic to help build trust with any prospect.*

This meeting agreement also helped Steve subtly take control of the sales interview without being pushy. It would

184

be done on his terms, but with the willing participation of his prospect, Mike.

Pre-Call Planning for the First Meeting With Solana

Steve knew the importance of planning his sales calls. He'd tried winging it, but found that when he took some time to determine his primary and secondary objectives for the call he got a lot more accomplished. First he went on Solana's website again to see what he could find. Specifically he was looking to gain a better understanding of Solana's business and to find out if there were any news items that they had posted on the site. His next stop was to look at Pacific's database to see if there was any call history that he could learn from. Then he pulled a D&B report to get some preliminary financial information.

Steve wanted to make sure he was focused for this call, so he took out his Common Sense Selling® Pre-Call Planning Worksheet and went to work.

He decided that his primary objective for the call was to find enough pain (critical widget related issues that he could help his prospect resolve) so that he would be justified in spending his time in putting together some preliminary ideas to discuss with Mike at a future meeting. But he certainly didn't want to go through the motions with little chance of success. He wrote a quick reminder to himself that he needed to test for commitment during the next meeting. Steve's secondary objective for the meeting, assuming he wasn't able to achieve his primary objective, was to begin to develop a personal relationship with Mike and Nancy in case their need to evaluate other widget suppliers was not critical so that he'd be considered for a future opportunity.

A few days passed and Steve was on the way to his appointment at Solana. It was about a 30-minute drive and he spent the time reviewing how he would start the call. He arrived in the parking lot ten minutes early and took a quick moment to review his Pocket Coach to remind himself of the qualifying questions that he wanted to ask during the meeting. He found that by doing this before and after every call he had become more and more comfortable with the Common Sense Selling® process and was able to remember the questions about pain, financial issues and decision process quite easily. As a result he had learned to qualify his opportunities more effectively.

The First Few Minutes of the Initial Face to Face Call

When Steve entered the lobby at Solana he introduced himself to the receptionist and said that he had a ten o'clock appointment with Mike and Nancy. He looked around the lobby to see if there was something that might be a good conversation topic when he arrived at Mike's office. There was an industry award on the wall that he decided to ask about.

Mike's earlier meeting took about ten minutes longer than was scheduled, so the meeting was going to start a few minutes late.

Sandy came down and escorted Steve up Mike's office. He was introduced to Nancy and after the usual pleasantries, Steve mentioned that he noticed the award that Solana had received and initiated a short discussion about the award.

After a couple of minutes of small talk Steve felt it was time to reconfirm the meeting agreement that he and Mike had discussed on the phone a few days before. He said, "Mike, when we spoke on the phone we agreed to spend about an hour on this meeting. Is that still good?" Mike replied that he did, indeed, have another meeting scheduled at 11:30am so they would need to adhere to the time frame.

Steve continued, "Well, then it's important that we stick to the agenda. As you might recall, this is really just a preliminary exchange of information to see if we even have a reason to consider developing a business relationship. Since I don't know much about your relationship with Delta and you don't know much about Pacific Widget, this is really just an opportunity to get to know each other. Hopefully at the end of the meeting we can decide together if it makes sense to talk further. As I mentioned on the phone if, for any reason, it doesn't, that's okay. And I appreciate the opportunity to ask you and Nancy some questions, and I'm sure you'll have some for me. I assume it's okay to take a few notes?"

Steve suggested that he start the meeting with a short overview of Pacific Widget. He limited his comments to a big picture overview of the company, let Mike know that he had other clients in his industry, but was careful not to make any self-serving claims about why Pacific would be the best supplier for Solana because he knew that those comments would be viewed with skepticism at this early stage of the relationship. This mini-presentation took about two minutes and avoided making any claims about being "the best" and other pufferies that would sound phony and cause Mike and Nancy to be skeptical.

Instead, he said, "I'd love to sit here and tell you that we're the best widget supplier for your company, but the fact is that I don't know that to be the case. Until I can determine what your needs are I'd just be overselling, and I try to stay away from that. It would help me, however, if you could tell me what you're looking for in a widget supplier and perhaps expand on the frustrations that you touched on when we spoke on the phone. Then at some point we can determine if we might have a fit. Okay?"

Mike thought, "Well, that's refreshing. He's not trying to pitch us on why he's the best supplier like every other salesperson that comes in here. Seems like a guy I can trust." He agreed to answer Steve's questions without hesitation.

Debrief

Steve's most important tactic during the first few minutes of the call was reviewing and reconfirming the Meeting Agreement. Notice that since the meeting started late he asked if he still had the full hour that was allotted. He made sure not to make any premature claims about his ability to help and made a special effort to reiterate that Mike and Nancy had every right to say "no" if they didn't feel further discussions, for whatever reason, were necessary. This is important if you are to set the appropriate tone for the meeting and, ultimately, the relationship.

Discovering the Prospect's Pain

Steve started by asking Mike to describe his relationship with Delta. "Tell me a little about your history with Delta," he said. Mike spent 2-3 minutes detailing Solana's history with Delta and how his company's growth and Delta's acquisition by Consolidated General had created some problems that was causing him to wonder if Delta Widget was the right supplier for Solana over the long term.

First of all, their long time rep had taken early retirement and he was not happy with his replacement. There were communication problems and the new rep simply didn't have the in-depth understanding of his business like the old one, and didn't seem to want to take the time to find out.

Secondly, Delta's warranty policy had changed for the worse. A more conservative atmosphere was a concern for Mike as his company was in a growth mode.

Steve summed up what Mike was telling him about the rep and warranty issues. He said, "I can understand why those would be concerns for you and I'd like to ask some questions about it, but before I do, are there any other issues that you're concerned about?"

Nancy spoke up, saying, "Steve, I agree with Mike about those things, but I'm concerned about the overall service and quality levels with Delta as well. Seems like the attention to detail that we've been used to just isn't as important to Delta these days. I think it has to do with their new owner's focus on the bottom line."

"I'm somewhat surprised to hear this about Delta actually. We find them to be a strong competitor in most instances," Steve remarked, attempting to remove pressure and test to see just how serious these issues were. He got the answer he was looking for when Nancy jumped in, saying, "Unfortunately that hasn't been our experience. A couple of my people are really frustrated."

"Why's that?" Steve asked. "Well," said Nancy, "with all the new policies and procedures we have to deal with lots of questions come up. They've got this customer support center but the 'support' is non-existent. It's only when I get on the phone and complain that we get any action."

"It can't be that bad," remarked Steve, again testing the severity of the situation.

"You don't know the half of it," said Nancy testily. "What sort of support does Pacific have?"

"Someone, a real body I mean, is always available 24/7 actually. I've never given it much thought. None of my clients have ever complained."

"That's good to hear," said Nancy. "I apologize, we got sidetracked there."

Steve said, "Okay, let me recap what I've heard so far. We've got the communication problem, the warranty issues and the service issues. Which one is the biggest concern for you?" Both Mike and Nancy agreed that the warranty issue was paramount.

Steve said, "Can you tell me more about why that's so important, Mike?"

"Well, as I said, Delta seems to have a more restrictive warranty policy these days, and with our growth and need for support with the components we use in our manufacturing process, widget failure and lack of warranty support could become a real problem for us."

"You mentioned widget failure. Has quality been a problem or is that just a part of the warranty issue?" asked Mike.

Nancy said that they were starting to notice a slight increase in the failure rate, and that was compounding their concerns about warranty problem.

"I see," said Steve. "Can you elaborate a little bit more about the warranty and quality situation?"

"Sure," said Mike. "Our business has been good over the past couple of years and there seems to be lots of opportunity out there for us. Problem is, it's a competitive business and quality and support is absolutely key for our customers. We believe that we have the best product on the market and our prices reflect that commitment to quality. If that's compromised by faulty components like widgets we really hear about it from our customers. Nancy and I are starting to get concerned that the new ownership at Delta might not have the same attention to quality and support that we've enjoyed in the past. And that's a real concern for us as we try to ramp up for some pretty aggressive growth."

"This sounds like a good opportunity for Delta, I mean with your growth plans and everything." replied Steve. "Seems like they'd be paying more attention to you, not less. Have there been any particular things that have happened with your customers that are causing concern?"

"Yes." said Mike. "Just the other day one of our largest customers called me and asked if there was anything going on with our product. Seems they had noticed a slightly higher failure rate and said the widgets were the problem. They said it was not a crisis situation, but when I get the call, you have to wonder how serious it might be. So, I'm curious, what can Pacific do for us?"

Steve thought for a moment. "Well, it appears that we could help, but it would be somewhat premature for me to start discussing our solutions until I have all the facts." he said. "Mind if I ask a couple more questions?"

"Sure, go ahead," Mike replied.

"Well, I assume you've spoken to Delta about your concerns and I think you said that they've been somewhat unresponsive so far. I'd guess that when their new rep gets his feet on the ground he'll take good care of you, wouldn't you think?"

Nancy jumped in. "I'd hope that would happen, but so far it doesn't look likely. I mean, although we're one of their larger customers, and what with their new management, maybe it's not realistic to hang our hopes on that happening. If we can't rely on them to be as responsive as they were in the past, we'll have to start looking for a better alternative. But, you know, it's really about finding a supplier that we can grow with. Certainly we need competitive prices, quality products and good service, but long term we need somebody who we can have a good relationship with. What do you think, Mike?" He agreed wholeheartedly.

Demonstrating good active listening skills, Steve said, "You just mentioned price, and this is the first time it's come up. Have they done anything with their prices since the takeover by Consolidated General?"

"No, they haven't," said Nancy. "But with their focusing more on their own bottom line, price increases might not be far behind. We're concerned about it."

"Suppose you can't find a more suitable supplier and have to stay with Delta. How would you feel about that?" asked Steve.

"If they don't clean up their act I think it would be very frustrating," said Nancy. "After all, it could restrict the growth plans we have. I know I'd be upset," she added.

"You mention growth plans," Steve said. "I don't mean to make any assumptions, but it sounds like your vendor partnerships are a pretty important part of your growth strategy. What does an ideal vendor partner for you look like?"

Mike and Nancy spent several minutes discussing how their vendors fit into their growth strategy, and it was starting to become clear that Delta was not passing the test with flying colors. He let them go on as he was obtaining valuable information that would help him position Pacific Widget as a strong candidate to win their business.

Continuing along the same line, Steve asked if anybody else in the organization was concerned about the situation with Delta. Mike replied, "You bet. Our senior staff, which includes four VP's and several directors who have been with us for a long time, are very concerned. You see, these folks' comp plans, bonuses and stock options are closely tied to our profitability and growth. Something like this could seriously impact their total compensation package, not to mention Nancy's, and mine of course. And if they started to look for other opportunities, we could be in big trouble. Their contributions are important and we're really a family here as well."

"I understand," said Steve. "In terms of priorities, I'm sure you've both got lots on your plates. What priority is resolving the widget situation you've described to me?"

"It's very important, for all the reasons we've discussed. I'd hate to see us with limited options in this area," replied Mike.

"Well, what were you hoping we could do for you," asked Steve.

Mike responded. "Here's what we're looking for. We need a supplier that can provide us with a viable alternative to Delta. Somebody whose quality is superior and who will stand behind their products and work with us as a partner. Nancy, what else is there?"

Nancy said, "Of course, the pricing has to be competitive as well. Don't you agree, Mike?"

Mike agreed, and added, "Are these things that Pacific can help us with, Steve?"

Steve thought for a moment before replying. "Certainly your business would be important to us. I think I understand what your requirements are. Let's pretend for a moment that we could come up with a plan that addressed all these issues satisfactorily, what would happen then?"

"Obviously we want to talk to several widget suppliers before we make any decisions to integrate someone else as an approved vendor. So it will be whoever has the best overall deal for us."

"When you say 'the best deal'," Steve asked, "what exactly does that mean? I guess my biggest concern is that at the end of the day will it be based primarily on price, notwithstanding the challenges you're having now with quality, warranty and communication. Because we're not likely to be the lowest price supplier out there."

Mike looked over at Nancy, who responded. "Of course price is important, and we need to be competitive, but we also recognize that you've got to be profitable in order to provide quality widgets and do all the other things we expect in a vendor."

Determining the Financial Details

Further questioning enabled Steve to determine that Solana purchased about 95% of their widgets from Delta, and used a small local manufacturer named Coast Widget for the balance. Coast was a quality supplier, but did not have the capacity to step in as a viable replacement for Delta and was not being considered for more business. Solana's annual purchases with Delta were in the two million dollar range.

Understanding the Decision-Making Process

Steve checked his watch and noticed that he had about ten minutes left before his hour was up. He knew that he had access to the right people in Mike and Nancy. But there was far more that he needed to know to completely understand the decision process so there weren't any loose ends that could sabotage his efforts. Specifically he still needed to know who was responsible for making the decision, when the decision needed to be made and why that date was important, what Mike and the other influencers would need to see from him so that they had all the information they needed to make a decision and, finally, if there were any roadblocks that might get in the way of getting a supplier change implemented. He'd already determined what criteria Solana would evaluate in order to select a widget supplier.

Steve initiated the discussion with one very simple question. "What process would you go through to make a decision to switch or bring on another widget supplier?"

Mike replied, "Nancy and I will be the decision makers on this. And, of course, we'll be talking to several companies. We want to get a good perspective on what's available out there."

"Makes sense," said Steve. "Will anyone else be involved? Your purchasing people possibly?"

"Actually, I'd want to have Bruce McCall involved. He's our Director of Purchasing and has been with the company for a long time. He reports to me and is very familiar with Delta," said Nancy. "We wanted him to be part of this meeting, but something came up at the last minute."

"That makes sense," said Steve. "When will I get a chance to speak to Bruce to find out what's important to him regarding widgets?" Nancy suggested that Steve call Bruce and that she would tell him to expect Steve's call.

"Terrific. I'm curious, however. How does Bruce feel about the situation with Delta? Since he's been here so long, I imagine he has some strong ties to them." Steve was deliberately trying to determine if Bruce was going to be a roadblock for him down the line. If he was, he wanted to know that as soon as possible so he could develop a strategy to address the problem.

Nancy explained that Bruce's recommendations would be valued since he was closest to the situation, and that she suspected that he had some strong loyalties to Delta. After all, they had always been good about taking him to golf outings and baseball games, since he was an avid sports fan. Steve was already starting to plan his strategy with Bruce based on her comments.

"I appreciate the info on Bruce, Nancy. Our time is getting short, and I just have a couple of other questions, if it's okay?" Steve continued. "When do you see yourselves making a decision regarding what you'll do about the widget situation?"

Nancy replied, "I'd guess that the whole evaluation process might take up to three months or so, so a good target for us to make the decision would be sometime early next quarter."

"Okay," said Steve. "Let me back up for a moment. You said that you'd be looking at several suppliers including, I assume, Delta. Have you received any proposals from anyone that looked attractive to you?"

"Actually," said Nancy, "our plan has been to look at three widget suppliers, including Delta. You'd be the fourth, but another proposal wouldn't hurt. But we haven't received any proposals yet."

Steve took a deep breath, and then said, "Can I say something without your getting upset at me?" He looked for affirmation, and received it. Then he continued. "Maybe I'm a little gun shy since this happened to me just a few weeks ago, but what's the likelihood of your just using these other proposals just to gain better leverage with Delta?"

Mike replied. "I understand your concern, Steve. I came up through the sales ranks myself, and never appreciated it when somebody did that to me. Our intention is not to spend a lot of time with various suppliers just to get a low-ball proposal to make Delta more responsive. Pricing is only one of the issues, as we've said. The problem goes deeper than price."

"Glad to hear that," said Steve, who <u>was</u> relieved. He watched their body language carefully when asked that question to make sure they weren't stretching the truth. Their reply seemed to be sincere.

Steve felt like he'd done a thorough job of understanding Mike and Nancy's widget challenges and they seemed motivated enough to seriously consider moving their business from Delta if the deal was right. But, based on his experience, he still had some misgivings.

Debrief

Clearly Steve had initiated his discussions with Solana at an opportune time, when they were having some serious doubts about their relationship with their widget supplier. Timing is everything, as they say.

Nevertheless, so far Steve has done a great job of investigating (qualifying) for the prospect's pain, money issues and decision process. He was able to uncover several pain issues (lack of communication due to a new sales rep, warranty and quality issues, and concern about the direction Delta was headed as a result of their new ownership.) His questioning process was conversational and he was able to determine how some of these issues affected the company as well as the individuals. He was successful in creating an atmosphere where Mike and Nancy were comfortable opening up and telling him what

196

was on their mind. They volunteered that the problems were serious and that it was not a good option to keep things the way they were. Finally, he was able to get them to paint a picture of their vision for a successful vendor relationship.

He determined their annual purchases and had made a mental note to ask Bruce to give him more specific information about the warranty situation. He found out their decision process; who would be involved, the time line for making a decision and their decision criteria which was very important since they would be looking at several vendors.

He also asked a critical question to make sure they were not planning to use his proposal simply to negotiate a better deal with Delta. That took guts, but he softened it with a third party story about how it had recently happened to him with another prospect so it didn't appear that he was accusing them of being unprofessional.

Dealing with Problems Up Front

Steve had been through many meetings such as this, and often found that when all was said and done, despite the apparent severity of the prospect's pain, it was a major hassle for companies to switch suppliers. He had heard this excuse before and wanted to find out just how serious they were about switching before he went to all the trouble of having additional meetings and spending time developing a proposal. So he said to Mike, "You know, there's one thing that I'm concerned about. Can I share it with you?"

Mike replied, "Of course. What is it?"

"Well," said Steve. "You've indicated that you have some fairly serious concerns about Delta, and that you'd consider leaving them if you felt the program was right for your company. And that's great, but switching suppliers can be a major undertaking and I'm concerned that we're both going to spend a lot of time and effort on this and that at the end of the day, you'll decide to stay with Delta simply because changing suppliers is such a hassle. What's the likelihood of that happening?"

"You make a good point," said Mike, "and we've already considered that. Yes, it is a hassle to change suppliers, but if we really feel that it's the right thing for Solana, we're willing to make the effort. Nancy, how do you feel about that?"

Nancy's department would have to shoulder the major burden of change, but she acknowledged that they would be agreeable to changing. Steve sensed some reluctance on her part, however, and felt that she might just be parroting the company line to avoid conflict with the CEO, so he said, "Are you sure, Nancy? You seem to have some concern."

"No," she replied. "I'd be willing to go through the discomfort if the program was right. They're starting to cause me some major headaches right now."

Based on their comments, Steve felt like they did, indeed, have enough issues with Delta to seriously consider making a change. He felt like this would be a good prospect to pursue and that he wouldn't get the ubiquitous "we've decided to stay put since it's such a hassle to change" excuse after a long courtship period.

They agreed that Steve's next step should be to contact Bruce McCall, the Director of purchasing, to set up a meeting. After that, he would call Mike to discuss what the next step should be.

After he left the meeting with Mike and Nancy he spent a couple of minutes in his car mentally debriefing what he did right and what he might have done better on the call. He jotted down a couple of additional notes that he wanted to remember before driving back to his office. He found that this exercise helped reinforce the Common Sense Selling® process he was using.

Debrief

Before he left he addressed the issue of the hassle of changing suppliers, an excuse that he and his sales colleagues had seemingly heard a thousand times after they had gone through a lengthy period of "courting" a prospect and the subsequent development of a proposal. That last minute objection, the hassle of changing, had cost him dearly over the years, but recently he had learned to address the "objection" up front. By getting the prospect to say that they understood it would be a hassle, but that they were willing to do it not only made Steve feel they were more committed, but also went a long way toward eliminating that objection later.

Using the Proposal Coach Software

Steve remembered that his training company had recently developed a short software program called the Proposal Coach that helped salespeople find out how effectively they had qualified a sales opportunity, and he did the assessment on his return to office. The 25 questions took only 8 minutes to complete and he got a five-page report filled with suggestions that he could implement. Certainly he had a long way to go, but he wanted to see what he had missed so he could find out those things on the next call. His score was only 38, which suggested that he had no better than a 38% chance of getting the business if he made a proposal now. Clearly, he still had some work to do, but the Proposal Coach report gave him a number of good suggestions for the next several meetings.

Fast Forward Several Weeks

Over the next couple of weeks Steve had one more meeting with Mike and Nancy as well as a meeting with Bruce McCall, the Director of Purchasing. These meetings were an important step in building additional rapport with the key people at Solana and qualifying the opportunity further – gaining a better understanding of their pain, their decision process and their purchasing priorities so that he could position his company successfully when the time came to present his solutions. Nancy had asked Steve for several references to speak with, and was comfortable with what they had to say about their relationship with Pacific and Steve.

Testing for Commitment and Setting the Stage for the Presentation

Steve was excited about the possibilities of winning Solana's business. He felt he'd qualified the opportunity thoroughly; he understood the supply issues they were trying to remedy and their decision process. He'd spent time getting to know the company and their key people and felt like he was as ready as he could be. He'd used the Proposal Coach software several times and his score was now 73, indicating that he had better than a 70% chance of getting the business. He felt about as confident as he could.

The next step was the formal proposal to Mike and Nancy. After they agreed on the date and time, Steve set the closing meeting agreement with Mike. This was a critical step in the process to insure that he continued to maintain control. His objectives were to make sure that everybody who needed to be a part of the decision process would be present, to demonstrate that Pacific could successfully address the problems that Solana was experiencing and to get a decision at the end of his presentation.

He said, "When we get together for the presentation the week after next, we'll need about an hour. Will that work for you?"

"No problem. That works for us," Mike replied.

"And can we make sure that everybody that needs to be present will be? That would be you and Nancy, of course. How about Bruce?"

"Yes, Bruce needs to be at the meeting. It will be the three of us," Mike replied.

"Great. And can you tell me what you'll need to see in the presentation so that you can be comfortable that you have all the information you need to make a decision on our proposal?" Mike told Steve what they'd be looking for in the way of proof, and Steve assured him that he'd be able to provide them with that information.

Steve knew he had to test again for commitment. He said, "Mike, assuming after my presentation you and Nancy have the conviction that my proposal is exactly what you need, and the numbers fit, what would happen then?"

Mike responded, "Well, I know you'd like to get a decision then, but we've got Lambert Widgets (another competitor) coming in the day after you. At that point we'll discuss the pros and cons of each and have a final decision by the 20th. We'll let you know then."

"I understand that you'll need some time," Steve said. "But could I ask a favor? At the end of my presentation could you tell me if there are any issues that would disqualify my proposal from being accepted?" Mike agreed that he and Nancy could do that.

Steve, of course, was disappointed that he would not get a decision at the end of his presentation. He knew that time killed deals, but he felt like he had done the best he could and knew that he had to respect Mike and Nancy's decision process. He was further comforted by the fact that he knew that decisions were often made long before the presentation was delivered, and that the formal proposal was in many ways simply a confirmation of what they had already agreed to. Thus, there would be no surprises in his presentation as they had agreed in advance that virtually all of his terms were acceptable to them. He felt like he had the inside track. Plus, he knew he could use a tactic called "The Scale" during the presentation to smoke out any resistance and find out exactly where he stood.

Debrief

Havting a good closing plan helped Steve insure he had ample time to make his presentation and he did a good job of "testing the waters" to try to find out what would happen if his presentation was exactly what his prospect was looking for. Notice that he asked an open-ended question ("what would happen then?") and not the more traditional closed-end question ("would we have a deal?") Although he didn't get the commitment he was looking for, at least he knew what would happen next. He also took the unusual step of asking if they would tell him if there was anything in the presentation that would disqualify him, thus giving him a chance to address any objections or concerns while he was still there.

Making the Presentation

When Steve arrived in the conference room for the presentation he reviewed the meeting agreement to make sure that nothing had changed. Mike, Nancy and Bruce were all there so he was relieved that they had kept their commitment to have all the decision makers and influencers present. He reviewed the issues that he was going to discuss (Solana's pains) and asked them to prioritize them. He tackled each issue in turn, making sure to confirm that his solution was totally acceptable to all of them before moving to the next one.

About two-thirds of the way through the presentation he decided to stop and see what kind of progress he was making. So far they seemed to be quite receptive, judging from their comments and body language. He decided to use "the scale" to see just how close he was to getting Solana's business.

He said, "Before I go any further, mind if I ask a question?"

"Sure," they replied.

"Well, I just want to check on our progress here. On a scale of one to ten, with ten being you're ready to accept our proposal right now and not even meet with Lambert Widget tomorrow, where are you?" He quickly added, "And I know you're not a ten," to take the pressure off.

Nancy looked at Mike, who smiled and nodded his head affirmatively. She said, "I'd say we're probably an eight, Steve. Your proposal is pretty much what we're looking for."

"That's great," Steve replied. "Looks like we're making some progress, but still have a way to go. What do you need to see so that it would be totally acceptable, you know, no reservations about going forward with us?"

Mike said, "Steve, I'm totally comfortable with your proposal. As I said, we still have to meet with Lambert. You're the leader in the clubhouse at this point, and that would include Delta since we've seen their proposal. What about you, Nancy?"

Nancy concurred with Mike and added, "I'm comfortable as well. Do you think it would be possible for us to have a tour of Pacific's plant sometime in the next week or so? We'd like to get to know your management team just a little before we make a final decision."

Steve agreed readily to Nancy's request feeling this was a strong expression of interest, and set up a visit for the following Wednesday morning. He made sure to find out exactly what Nancy wanted to accomplish during the visit so he could relate that to the management team at the plant. He felt strongly that if the tour were successful they would have the inside track on the business.

Steve covered the last few items on the list and said, "Well, what should I do now?" Mike suggested he call on the 20th for their decision after Nancy had a chance to tour the plant. He complimented Steve on his hard work and said he felt very comfortable with his knowledge of their business and attention to detail.

Before Steve left, he decided to ask one more question. This one took some guts, but considering the positive vibes he was getting he decided that the risk was certainly worth the reward. He said, "Before I leave, can I ask just one more question?" They agreed.

He took a deep breath. "You said that I was the frontrunner at this point, but you still have to see what Lambert comes in with. I'm curious, what are you hoping they will propose that would knock me out of the race?"

Their answer was just what he wanted to hear. "Steve, we can't think of anything, unless, of course, they beat your pricing by a bunch, but you're very competitive and from what they've told us, your proposal will hold up nicely. And as we've said, this is not just about pricing."

Steve felt relieved. He agreed to call on the 20th after the plant tour to get their decision. He added that he hoped to be chosen but if at that time they felt that his proposal was not the best one for them he was comfortable with them "telling him no."

He drove off back to his office, all the while debriefing how the meeting had gone. He decided it went about as well as he could have hoped for. The only unknown was what Lambert would do. He wondered if he should have asked for "last look" just in case. He'd done that on occasion, but somehow he felt that it might imply that he could go lower on his pricing and he felt that, all things considered, that was a bad strategy.

Two weeks passed and although the plant tour went well Steve went through the typical range of emotions that most salespeople go through – from total optimism to complete self-doubt. But this was normal.

Debrief

Steve delivered a great presentation. He reviewed the issues, prioritized them and addressed them one by one, being sure to get Mike and Nancy's approval on each before moving to the next. He used the scale, a great tactic to discover the prospect's level of acceptance, and although he didn't get to the ten he was hoping for, got enough positive feedback that he felt like when they said he was the front runner, he really was. He asked a very courageous question about what Lambert might show them that would knock him out of the race and was more than satisfied with their answer. And, he established a clear next step to get a final decision.

The Decision and Protecting the Sale

Steve called Mike on the 20th for his decision as agreed. Sandy took his call and Steve listened for any clues her tonality. Fortunately, it seemed positive and she was very friendly. He relaxed somewhat. He had gotten to know Sandy fairly well over the past few weeks and he felt like he was pretty good at reading people, but this was crunch time and he was nervous. Sandy put him through.

Before Steve could say a word Mike said, "Steve, we've decided to go with you guys. When can we get the transition started?"

Whoa, thought Steve. That was fast. Total relief overcame him. It was all worthwhile. He had won. Reflexively, he remarked, "That's a relief to me, obviously. I'm curious though, what was it that convinced you that we were the right company for you?"

Mike's answer surprised him. "Steve, you asked the best questions. No one else seemed to take the time or, for that matter, care much about what our real issues were. The others seemed to feel it was all about price, and it wasn't. We felt like we'd just be getting into another mediocre supplier relationship like the one we had before. That's why we picked you. Our only hope was that you wouldn't blow it with your proposal, and, of course, you didn't. It really was yours to lose. "

Although relieved, Steve knew from experience that the business was not secure until he had tested for any buyer's remorse and discussed competition's possible response.

This was the final step in the sales process, an insurance policy that all his hard work wouldn't unravel at the last minute. His experience was that while this tactic seemed risky to rookies, he'd had nothing but positive response to it.

He said to Mike, "I'm really glad that you decided to give us your widget business. I'll do everything that I can to make sure the transition is a smooth one and look forward to being your supplier for a long time. I want to make sure that you both are totally comfortable with your decision. Any reservations whatsoever? I mean, this is, after all, a big decision."

They responded, "No, Steve, we think this will work out well for us. We're comfortable with our decision."

"You're sure?" he added.

"Absolutely," said Mike.

Okay, one down and one to go, thought Steve. Competition – the final hurdle. He knew he had to go for it or risk losing everything just before the finish line.

"I'm pleased to hear that," said Steve. "But, you know, there's one thing that I'm still a little concerned about. Mind if I discuss it with you?"

"What's that?" replied Mike.

206

"Well, I guess I'm still concerned about how Delta might respond when they find out that you're moving your business to us. What do you think they'll do?"

"Oh, I suppose they'll try to come back in and start cutting price or offering some inducements to stay with them," said Mike.

"I'm sure they will. That would make sense," replied Steve. "I'm curious, if they do that what will you do?"

Mike took this one and answered forcefully, "They had their chance. They weren't there when we needed them and a little price-cutting isn't going to change our minds. We're anxious to get started with you folks."

Steve felt a sigh of relief. He had cleared the last hurdle. They had told him they wouldn't buckle under when Delta came back begging for a second chance. He knew that once someone had been asked to address that issue and volunteered that any competitive retaliation would not be successful, they normally stood behind their word. He made arrangements with Mike and Nancy to come out the following week and begin the transition process.

Debrief

Mike's answer to Steve's well-placed question about why they chose him was significant, and illustrates the importance of asking questions to understand the prospect's pain (or critical business issues.) People often make their buying decisions, or at least develop strong buying preferences, before the salesperson makes a presentation. It's been proven time after time that the best investigators close the most business. This is an important lesson to learn.

Protecting the sale after the client has made a commitment to buy is critical if you want to avoid problems like buyer's remorse, competitive retaliation and other roadblocks that have the potential to derail all your hard work. Steve handled both in textbook fashion and while, to the untrained eye, it appeared he was giving them an "out," just the opposite happened – they reaffirmed their desire to do business with him. This is an important, but underused, tactic. You'd do well to make it a permanent part of your selling repertoire.

Conclusion

It would be great to say this was the end of the story, and "they all lived happily ever after," but, in fact, the hard work was just beginning. Steve knew that now his *new* client, Solana, was now his competition's best prospect. He knew that he would have to avoid making the mistake Delta made by taking Solana's business for granted. He started to think about ways he could keep Solana satisfied. He understood that "satisfaction" was a function of anticipated results versus actual results. In other words, he'd have to under promise and over deliver as much as possible. He resolved to meet with them frequently with the specific purpose of soliciting bad news so he could address any issues before they became big problems. In order to encourage open communication he introduced Mike and Nancy to Mary Davis, his VP of Sales and said that if they ever had any problems with him personally they should feel comfortable calling Mary directly.

Three months into the new relationship Steve determined from Mike and Nancy that they were completely satisfied with their decision to move their business to Pacific Widget. He asked for referrals and was rewarded with two personal introductions to companies that fit his key prospect profile perfectly. The sales process began anew with the two referrals.

And that's the end of the story!

Straight Talk from the Authors

*"You must be in tune with the times and
be prepared to break with tradition."*
William Agee, writer

Your selling world is changing, and you must change with it, or suffer the consequences. If you keep doing things the same way, you can't expect your results to change. Working harder doesn't work, especially if your basic approach is flawed. Yet most salespeople are highly resistant to change even when they know what they are doing isn't achieving the desired level of success.

If your sales approach doesn't evolve, if you can't make the transition from product pusher to solution provider, you'll never be considered a trusted advisor and you won't enjoy the considerable rewards that accrue to the top echelon of sales professionals.

The question is, are you ready for a change, are you ready to increase your income substantially, or are you merely content with the status quo? Change is risky. Perhaps you're afraid to step out of your comfort zone. Many are. Nevertheless, the future...*your future* is predictable. There will be change. Those that change with it will grow. Those that do not will be left behind.

Let me leave you with these thoughts:

- Selling as a career provides the potential for virtually unlimited income.
- If you can really sell, you will be immune to the job frustrations faced by most Americans.
- Commit yourself to becoming a student of selling. The more you know, the more successful you will be.
- If you think that education is expensive, try ignorance.

- Your income can only grow to the extent that *you* grow.
- If you want to be paid the best, you've got to be the best. There are no shortcuts.
- You will be paid in direct proportion to the value you bring to your clients.

The choice is yours. Make the right one.

About the Authors

Jim Dunn and John Schumann are the principals of SalesCoach, LLC. Both have extensive experience selling, managing sales forces and training salespeople. Their approach to the sales process is a combination of the best practices in selling today.

They can be reached at 800-235-2816.

For information about the Common Sense Selling® training programs and products that are available, visit our website...www.whetstonegroup.com.